defining moments

defining moments

a journey to the ends of the earth and back   VERNON BREWER

BOOKS

PUBLISHED BY WORLD HELP, INC. FOREST, VIRGINIA

Cover and interior art by Roark Creative, www.roarkcreative.com

Copyright 2008 World Help. Printed in the United States of America.

ISBN 978-0-9788041-3-9

World Help
1148 Corporate Park Drive
Forest, VA 24551
worldhelp.net

World Help exists to fulfill the Great Commission and the Great Commandment through partnering, training, helping and serving, especially in the unreached areas of the world.

Dedicated to my heroes around the world . . . our national partners. Their tireless work to build the Kingdom, even in the face of great opposition and persecution, challenges me to never lose sight of the vision . . . to take the Gospel *to the ends of the earth and back*!

To my wife and children. Patty, thank you for being so supportive of my *ends of the earth* journeys. Noel, Nikki, Jenny, and Josh, thank you for catching God's vision and for your passion to make a difference.

To my grandchildren—Riley, Bentley, Adam, and Colin. Thank you for bringing so much joy, excitement, and laughter into my life. My prayer for you is that someday when you grow up, you will find God's *defining moments* for your life.

To my parents Fred and Vivian Brewer and my uncle Roscoe Brewer. Thank you for giving me a passion for ministry and a heart for the world.

To my World Help family. I am so fortunate to go to work every day with people I love and together accomplish something that will outlive us all and last for eternity.

contents

foreword

No one really knows why God chooses some people to have a greater impact on our world than others. It is a mystery for which I believe we won't truly have an answer until we get to heaven. I believe Vernon Brewer is one of those special people chosen by God to impact the world with the Gospel in remarkable ways. I am privileged to know him and to continue to see God greatly at work in Vernon's life.

I grew up in the household of another one of those special people: my dad, Jerry Falwell. Dad worked closely with Vernon through the years as they jointly sought new ways to reach the world for Christ. I had the great privilege of traveling with both of them to the far corners of this world in pursuit of this noble effort. It was through these travels, as well as God's calling on my life, that I began to see the importance of having a global vision—rather than just a local vision.

Recently, I was talking to Dr. Elmer Towns, the co-founder of Liberty University, about my father's heaven-inspired vision. Elmer shared a few words in that conversation that will forever be emblazoned on my heart. He said, "Your dad was probably the only person I ever met who had a great desire to reach the world for Christ, and was actually crazy enough to believe that he could do it." In my estimation, Vernon Brewer is in that same category. Like my father, he has an audacious, almost fearless, faith.

Like Dad and Vernon, I have a desire to cultivate a new generation of young people that has an unquenchable passion to reach the world for Christ. Wouldn't it be amazing to see a generation of Jerry Falwells and Vernon Brewers who were also "crazy enough" to believe they could actually pull off a quest to alter the course of their generation with the Gospel?

Vernon's book is a powerful story that details what the author has faced in his lifelong journey to reach the world for Christ. Some of these stories I personally witnessed; others I have read for the first time in these pages. All are stories of God's power and amazing grace.

This book is important because I firmly believe that Christians are at a spiritual crossroads. From the very first days of the church two thousand years ago, we have seen God's hand moving in powerful ways. However, I believe the days ahead are possibly the most critical. There is an insidious movement in our world that seeks to silence the voices of Christians. People within this movement do not want to see a new generation of Jerry Falwells and Vernon Brewers arise. Their desire is to stop the very hand of God.

Now is the time for all of us who claim the name of Christ to rise up as champions for Him. We must never allow our voices to be silenced, our passion to be diminished or our vision to be darkened. We must not be ashamed of the Gospel or timidly back away from tough cultural challenges. I hope you will read Vernon Brewer's powerful testimony herein and realize that the same God who has walked with him is the same God who walks with you.

Mark 10:27 says: *"Jesus looked at them and said, 'With man this is impossible, but not with God; all things are possible with God.'"* When we realize that our God is all-powerful and that all things are possible with Him, we too can be "crazy enough" to believe that we can change the world. Let's decide to do just that. Who knows what might happen!

Jonathan Falwell
Jonathan Falwell
Senior Pastor
Thomas Road Baptist Church
Lynchburg, Virginia

introduction

We each have what we call *defining moments* in our life. Those moments that seem to determine everything else that follows. Those moments that lay the groundwork for what we will do with the rest of our lives.

Mine came on the dusty roads of Mexico when I was just a teenager—and the moments never stopped.

When diagnosed with cancer at the age of 38, I thought my life was literally over—especially my ministry. When God healed me, I realized that my most important work was not *before* cancer, but *after*. I realized God was not finished with me yet.

Since then, I have determined to live my life in such a way that every day I try to accomplish at least one thing that will outlive me and last for eternity. God has literally taken me *to the ends of the earth and back*, to see this vision realized.

I pray that each of these very personal stories from the pages of my life will encourage, inspire, and challenge you to find your *defining moments* as well.

Vernon Brewer

CHAPTER ONE

regalo . . . gratis . . . suyo

"THERE ARE MANY THINGS IN LIFE THAT WILL CATCH
YOUR EYE, BUT ONLY A FEW WILL CATCH YOUR HEART
. . . PURSUE THOSE!"

—ANONYMOUS

I knocked on the door of the small straw and mud house, and quickly went over the words in my head, *"Regalo . . . Gratis . . . Suyo. Regalo . . . Gratis . . . Suyo."* These three Spanish words, learned only moments before, had yet to really impress me. At this point, they were only words. I would be lucky if I could just say them correctly.

The door slowly opened. My heart was pounding. The timid Mexican woman on the other side seemed puzzled as to why this young American boy stood at her door. What did he want? She lived in a small village, somewhat off the beaten path. She didn't receive many visitors, especially Americans.

In broken Spanish, I quickly mumbled the words I had memorized, *"Regalo Gratis Suyo"*—"Free gift for you." As the woman's face turned from suspicion to delight, I handed her a red New Testament in her own language.

This was my first mission experience. I was only 17 and fresh out of high school when my uncle Roscoe Brewer invited me on a youth mission trip to a little village in Mexico. Our group planned to construct a church building in a remote area where there were no churches of any kind. I had never traveled to a foreign country and couldn't imagine living in an area without a church. Neither could I envision a place where so many people had never seen a Bible. But as we traveled into the heart of Mexico, I knew I was traveling to such a place—an area of poverty, distress, and need.

By the time we arrived, the missionaries had already begun the construction process by pouring the foundation of a church building that would hold 300 people. Together, we laid concrete blocks and my job was to mix the cement in a wheelbarrow. My uncle taught me how to use a trowel and mortar to lay brick blocks and make sure they were level. I had never done anything like that in my life, much less in a foreign country.

One by one, we placed each block, battling the intense heat. Other group members made wooden trusses for the roof and prepared sheets of tin to nail down. The girls nailed wooden boards together to make benches for the congregation. When we finished the block work, stucco finish and whitewash were applied to the building. We strung electrical wire and hung bulbs from the ceiling for light. It was a crude and primitive building, but the villagers and the new young pastor took great pride in it.

We started working on the building on Monday morning, and by Friday night we dedicated this new church with several hundred people in attendance and many coming to faith in Christ.

We built the church in the mornings while the weather was cooler, and in the afternoons we took boxes of paperback Spanish New Testaments to the village slums. We delivered them door to door. I remember the dirt roads with open sewage running in front of houses and children playing outside the dilapidated shacks. Many wore no clothes. It was the worst poverty I had ever seen, the worst smells I had ever smelled. I was completely out of my comfort zone—confronted with great human need. I was emotionally drained and stretched beyond my limits.

Who would've thought knocking on doors, speaking the only words I knew in Spanish, "*Regalo Gratis Suyo*," and handing someone a New Testament would change my life? Seeing their eyes light up when they realized what they were receiving, and watching them hug the Bibles or even kiss them was indescribable. Sometimes they hugged and kissed me too.

I continued this process for a week. Some encounters led to salvation, and others we planted a seed; but each one tested my idea of the meaning of life. As each person took the Bible from my hands, important principles were embedded in my heart and mind forever—the power of God's Word, the joy of holding it, the privilege of owning a copy, and the need to share it.

On Friday night, many of those same villagers came to the church dedication with the red New Testaments in their hands. They heard the Gospel presented—some for the very first time. I was asked to share my testimony that night. As I looked out into the crowd, I saw how proud those villagers were to have a church of their own—a place to worship. I was overwhelmed with emotion. I watched as they proudly held their New Testaments while worshipping in the new church. I saw so many people come to faith and realized that a church had been established where only five days before, none had existed. What a huge impression these people had made on my life. One that I have never forgotten.

At the age of 17, I realized several things:
- Many people have never even held a copy of the Bible, let alone owned one
- How precious the Word of God is and how much I take it for granted
- How important it is to have a place to worship—a church to call your own

I don't think it's any coincidence that now, many years later,

I'm still traveling the world, facilitating construction of modest village church buildings, and distributing "free gifts" to people who have never owned a Bible.

Little did I know, as a 17-year-old young man, God was preparing me for what He wanted me to do with the rest of my life. I thought it would just be a fun youth trip to another country, but God used it to change the direction of my life.

A few years later, I went back to Mexico with my uncle. This time I was a new youth pastor myself, serving in my first church. I had married and our first child was on the way.

I took my youth group to the village of Allende where we built and dedicated a church building and distributed more than 22,000 New Testaments in one week. Over 600 people came to the dedication, and 139 came to faith in Christ. Of those American young people in our youth group, 26 made commitments to the ministry during that week. Today, many of them are still serving as missionaries and pastors around the world.

Catullus, the Roman poet, once said, "It is difficult to lay aside a confirmed passion."[1] Although methods and strategies have changed through the years, I have never been able to "lay aside" the passion God gave me for reaching the world with the Gospel.

Every one of us has *defining moments*. My moment came on a dirty, dusty village road in the heart of Mexico when I was only 17.

CHAPTER TWO

you have cancer

"GOD WHISPERS TO US IN OUR PLEASURES, SPEAKS IN OUR CONSCIENCE, BUT SHOUTS IN OUR PAINS; IT IS HIS MEGAPHONE TO ROUSE A DEAF WORLD."

—C.S. LEWIS[2]

Wednesday evening, May 1, 1985, was the most difficult night of my life. I had just endured a lengthy surgery where doctors discovered and removed a five-pound tumor that was attached to my heart and lungs.

Later, the medical staff told me if they had waited one more week to operate, it would have been too late. I was 38 years old, and my happy, busy life suddenly came to a grinding halt.

Over and over I replayed the scene in my mind and heard the doctor's fateful words—"You have cancer."

I was diagnosed with a rapidly growing form of Hodgkin's disease—a rare, malignant cancer affecting the lymphatic tissue in my body.

In that initial surgery, the doctors took out approximately one-third of my left lung in order to remove the entire tumor, but they inadvertently severed the nerve to my vocal cords and diaphragm.

The severed nerve made the simple task of speaking extremely difficult. I was forced to talk in whispers for the next year and a half. The doctors tried to give me hope by saying my vocal cords might heal in time. All I knew was I couldn't preach without a voice.

During the months that followed, I endured 18 additional surgeries and surgical procedures. I spent weeks at a time in the hospital, a year and a half of debilitating radiation and chemotherapy, countless, agonizing hours in physical therapy, and many days near death.

There were good days and bad days, lonely and dark days, and nearly every one of them was painful.

And then after months of excruciating pain and fear, the doctors gave me great news—they told me I would survive.

But, just when I thought it was all over—as if facing cancer and chemotherapy were not enough—I developed more complications. The vein in my hand where I received powerful drugs collapsed and produced a chemical burn that destroyed the tissue and tendons of the entire upper part of my left hand. Doctors had to once again operate immediately.

The plan was to do a simple skin graft. When I woke up, I discovered the problem was much more serious than they expected. They had to attach my hand to skin and tissue from my side for a month in order for the blood vessels to reconnect. So picture this . . . a grown man with the voice of a 6-year-old child, walking around with his hand attached to his side and stuck down the front of his pants. God has to have a sense of humor!

After numerous skin grafts and liposuction to make my hand look as normal as possible, the raised scar still serves as a daily reminder of the gift of life and how God brought me through the ordeal.

Finally, through the miracle of modern medicine, doctors injected liquid Teflon into my vocal cords, enabling me to speak.

I soon came to believe that God was going to do incredible

things through this trial in my life, but He had to teach me some things about myself. I believed He was going to heal me, and I believed He was going to use me and my struggles to change lives—I just didn't know how. But, God did.

CHAPTER THREE

village of grass huts

"JESUS REACHED OUT HIS HAND AND TOUCHED THE EYES OF THE BLIND, THE SKIN OF THE PERSON WITH LEPROSY AND THE LEGS OF THE CRIPPLE . . . JESUS KNEW LOVE USUALLY INVOLVED TOUCHING."

—DR. PAUL BRAND[3]

Wash your hands often, be careful what you eat, what you touch, and remember your immune system is compromised—just be careful." After much persuasion and arm twisting, my doctors reluctantly agreed to let me go, but not without plenty of warnings and shots.

There was a famine in Africa with thousands starving to death in the Sudan and Ethiopia. The world was uniting to do something to help, and I had been on the sidelines far too long.

I had just survived a nearly two-year battle with cancer. My immune system was weak, which made me susceptible to colds, the flu, and every other disease. I still felt like life was passing me by and I had to make up for lost time. So, off I went to see what difference I could make.

At the time, I was vice president of Liberty University, and we were taking a team of faculty and students to Africa. I had no idea what the outcome would be—I just knew I had to do something.

After arriving in Nairobi, Kenya, we chartered a small single-engine plane and flew north past the equator to the Sudan border and landed on a gravel runway. In the distance, I could see a village of grass huts. I had never seen a village like that before, except in *National Geographic*. So of course, I was intrigued.

As we got off the plane, it was over 100 degrees—the unbearable heat and humidity took our breath away. We were met by an African pastor, and I asked him whether we had time to visit the village and take some photos (that's what Americans do on the mission field . . . they take photos).

Because of the famine and drought, there was no fresh water anywhere. I was told large trucks had to bring water in every day from as far away as 80 kilometers. It was sobering to see tribal women on their knees, digging with their bare hands in dry riverbeds, trying to find water. The pastor said, "They won't find any water, but if they do, it will probably be contaminated and do them more harm than good."

We arrived at the village only to find it deserted—not a soul in sight. I began taking photos, snooping around, and I actually went up to one of the huts. It didn't have a door, only an opening with an animal-skin covering. I stuck my head in to look around and was shocked to see a little girl, maybe 9 years old, standing just inside in the doorway. All she was wearing was a dirty pair of underpants. She was filthy! Her hair was matted, her nose running, and her belly distended—showing early signs of malnutrition. She had open sores all over her body and the smell was awful. All I could think about was my doctors' parting words, "Be careful what you touch." I was so repulsed I took a giant step backward and froze.

At that moment, I didn't hear an audible voice, but I did hear the Spirit of God quietly chasten me, "Wait just a minute. Who do you think you are? Do you see that little girl? I love her just as

27

much as I love your girls back home. I love that little girl so much, I sent my Son to die for her . . . and I have commanded you to love her too." I was immediately humbled and convicted.

Partly out of guilt and partly out of impulse, I reached forward and picked up that dirty, smelly little girl and held her tight in my arms. I later found out I was the first white person she had ever seen, so I'm sure I scared her to death. I couldn't speak her language and she couldn't speak mine. But I held her, touched her cheek, and tried my best to show her I cared.

What happened next is still hard to believe after all these years. While I was holding that dirty, destitute child, out from the hut came her mother, father, brothers and sisters, and even her grandparents. I didn't realize so many people could fit inside one hut. Not only did the hut empty out, but within minutes, I was surrounded by everyone in the village—several hundred starving and thirsty nomadic Turkana Africans.

I saw an elderly woman who was blind, a man with a tumor on his neck—obviously terminal—and another man whose leg was swollen three or four times its normal size. I looked into the eyes of the diseased, blind, and lame. For the first time in my life, I realized what Jesus must have felt when he saw the crowds and *"was moved with compassion for them."*[4]

I felt so helpless in the face of such great human suffering and need. I asked the pastor if he had anything we could give them. He said he had a case of corn meal in the back of his vehicle—and he willingly gave it to me. We were able to give each family one five-pound bag. You would have thought it was Christmas morning. Everyone was smiling and laughing. They thanked me and some even hugged me. It left an indelible memory.

The African villagers told me their greatest need was water— they were dying. I had the opportunity to give words of encouragement and hope. And as the pastor interpreted, I also shared the good news of the Gospel. I told the pastor we had to do more, and I asked him to drive me to the district governmental offices. The officials described the crisis. They needed to drill wells immediately if they were going to save lives. I didn't even know what it cost to drill a well, but the words were out of my mouth: "We will do it. By faith, we will do it!"

When I returned to Liberty University, I shared the need and my experiences. I challenged students to do something bigger than themselves—to make a difference in someone else's life, to be moved with compassion. I wasn't prepared for their response. The money for the wells was raised in one week, and the life-giving water soon began to flow.

They gave their money, but they also gave of their lives. Ten students stepped up and committed to take a semester out of school to go to Northern Kenya. They would oversee the drilling of the wells, establish a medical clinic, and plant a church. At the end of that semester, 10 more students took their place, and the next semester another 10, and then another 10. Three years later, the wells and the medical clinic had saved hundreds of lives, and the church had witnessed the salvation of many people. Everyone in that village became a Christ follower during that three-year period, and their lives and mine would never be the same. Beyond that, hundreds of students did something that would last for eternity.

That day, in the middle of grass huts, God taught me compassion. Most of us consider compassion as simply feeling sorry for someone or having a mild touch of pity for someone, but the Bible defines compassion as much more than that. When Jesus *"was moved with compassion,"* it wasn't just pity; it literally was *"suffering together with someone."* That's what Jesus did. He suffered with them. Pity sees and even feels, but compassion touches the need. He held the children, He touched the lepers, and He touched the blind man's eyes. When Jesus was confronted with great human need—death, disease, hunger, and the plight of the homeless—He was always moved with compassion.

At the end of the Korean War, evangelist Billy Graham and Robert Pierce, founder of World Vision, were faced with the dilemma of thousands of homeless, orphaned children. Pierce made a statement that is now famous: "Let my heart be broken with the things that break the heart of God." That's my favorite definition of compassion.

Apart from the Spirit of God, I am not a compassionate person, so I find myself regularly, sometimes daily, praying, "Lord, let my heart be broken with the things that break Your heart." When I do, my mind goes back to a little girl in Africa and a village of grass huts.

CHAPTER FOUR

mr. gorbachev,
tear down this wall

"YES, ACROSS EUROPE, THIS WALL WILL FALL. FOR IT CANNOT WITHSTAND FAITH; IT CANNOT WITHSTAND TRUTH. THE WALL CANNOT WITHSTAND FREEDOM."

—RONALD REAGAN[5]

On June 12, 1987, President Ronald Reagan stood at the Berlin Wall, the defining symbol of the Cold War, and spoke those words which are now famous, "Mr. Gorbachev, tear down this wall."

Only two years later, the once unthinkable happened. The wall came down.

I was in Budapest, Hungary, with a group of 57 Liberty University students. We boarded the train to Oradea, Romania, a five-hour ride. For most of the students, it would be their first visit to a communist country.

When we arrived at the Romanian border, our car was detached from the train and placed on a different track. We sat there for more than 14 hours without food, water, or heat. Many of the students were frightened, to say the least.

The former Soviet Union was unraveling, and Romanian dictator Nicolae Ceausescu didn't want what was happening in Moscow and Berlin to happen in Romania. He ordered Romania's borders closed to all foreigners. We were stuck.

After a cold night, workers reattached our train car to an outbound train and we were on our way back to Budapest. As we pulled out of the station, one of the girls was crying. I asked her if she was sad because she could not visit Romania. "No," she said, "I'm sad because I now see the persecution that the Romanian people live with every day."

It reminded me of my first visit to Communist Romania. I was detained at the border and my camera, Bible, and sermon notes were confiscated. I never got them back. We were followed by the secret police everywhere we went, and after we left, the Romanian pastors we visited were arrested and interrogated—only because we had been there.

In spite of great persecution, we found Christ followers who were totally committed to Jesus Christ. They attended early morning prayer meetings and packed into the outdated church buildings five times a week. Hundreds stood in the aisles. They had so little, living near poverty, but they loved God so much.

One church I visited was scheduled for bulldozing by the government to make room for a high-rise apartment building. The night before it was scheduled for demolition, the congregation locked themselves in the church building and prayed all night. Amazingly, the next day the soldiers left and the building was saved. A few months later, Billy Graham spoke at that same church. There were more than 35,000 people there to hear him.

One early Sunday morning in Romania, my friend Pastor Cornel Iova picked me up in his car. We were going to visit a village church several hours away in the mountains.

As I sat in the back seat, Pastor Iova said, "Today is a very special day for me." When I asked why, he replied, "Today is the first anniversary of the death of my wife." Sympathetically, I asked how she died.

"Cancer," he said. He knew I was a cancer survivor.

He told me his wife was diagnosed by a group of doctors who

had visited Romania from the United Kingdom. They offered to bring her to London to perform the delicate bone marrow transplant surgery that could not be done in Romania at the time. They would pay for all the expenses. All she needed was a visa to leave the country.

When she went to the government office to apply for the visa, they knew she was a pastor's wife. The communist authorities told her they would give her a visa if she renounced her faith in Jesus Christ. I was shocked.

"What did she say?" I asked.

"She didn't hesitate for one instant. She said, 'I cannot and I will not do what you ask me to do,'" Pastor Iova said. "With her head held high, she walked out of that office." A few minutes later, he added, "Within two months she was gone."

I could not comprehend that level of commitment. I had no idea what to say. I simply told him how sorry I was.

After several moments of silence, he added, "Today is a special day for another reason." He explained that the village church we were visiting was conducting their first baptismal service in more than 50 years. In fact, the government had sent soldiers to demolish the church three times, and all three times the church members rebuilt the building. Cornel told me there would be 21 candidates for baptism and that I would share the Gospel with the entire village.

When we arrived, I found the church packed to capacity. All the family members of the baptismal candidates were there, and almost everyone in the village was present. Some of the youth wired the houses of villagers with closed circuit T.V. so those who were unable to attend could view the service. Cornel was right. I preached the Gospel to the entire village. That day we saw more than 62 new Christ followers, and that remote Romanian village was changed forever.

When the train, filled with those 57 students, returned to Budapest, I left them in the care of my lifelong friend John Lloyd, and I caught the first flight to Berlin. The Iron Curtain was coming down. German youth were dancing on the Berlin Wall in celebration, and I wanted to be there.

When my flight landed, I asked the taxi driver to take me straight to the Brandenburg Gate. It was late at night, but the party was still going strong. I met a German student who had a hammer and chisel; he was chipping off pieces of the wall as souvenirs. I offered him five dollars for his tools and within minutes, I, too, was chipping at the wall. I also bought a can of spray paint and painted my name on the Berlin Wall—"Vernon was here."

A few months later, I was back in Romania with Jerry Falwell and Mark DeMoss. It was their first visit to a communist country. We were invited to speak at the Communist Congress Palace in Bucharest where dictators ruled with an iron fist. The place was packed that night with more than 4,000 people, and most of them had never heard the Gospel. Before the night was over, 300 became Christ followers.

Since my first trip to Romania, I have visited at least 38 times. I never realized then what I know full well now. Romania was on the brink of revolution and unprecedented religious freedom. The walls were torn down. The world would never be the same.

CHAPTER FIVE

a 5-year-old boy
that changed my life

"LOUIS PASTEUR, THE PIONEER OF IMMUNOLOGY, LIVED AT A TIME WHEN THOUSANDS OF PEOPLE DIED EACH YEAR OF RABIES. PASTEUR HAD WORKED FOR YEARS ON A VACCINE. JUST AS HE WAS ABOUT TO BEGIN EXPERIMENTING ON HIMSELF, A [YOUNG CHILD], JOSEPH MEISTER, WAS BITTEN BY A RABID DOG. THE BOY'S MOTHER BEGGED PASTEUR TO EXPERIMENT ON HER SON. PASTEUR INJECTED JOSEPH FOR 10 DAYS—AND THE BOY LIVED. DECADES LATER, AFTER HAVING ACCOMPLISHED SO MUCH, PASTEUR ASKED FOR THESE THREE WORDS TO BE ETCHED ON HIS HEADSTONE: 'JOSEPH MEISTER LIVED.'

OUR GREATEST LEGACY WILL BE THOSE WHO LIVE ETERNALLY BECAUSE OF OUR EFFORTS."

—R. WAYNE WILLIS[6]

"If you want to catch fish, you must go where the fish are." A Brazilian pastor shared this concept with me as he explained that more than 500,000 people traveled by boat every day to and from work across the bay near Rio de Janeiro. We got permission to set up our sound equipment and instruments on the back of a flatbed trailer and parked it next to the boat docks. We roped off a large area in front of the stage and waited for the crowds to come. Every 30 minutes, more than 20 large ferries with over 5,000 people each pulled into the docks.

It was the summer of 1988, and I had traveled to Brazil with my family and an eager group of Liberty University students to distribute Bibles, visit children's homes, and present concerts in public schools, churches, and outdoor plazas. We even built a children's center in one of the worst slums in all of Rio.

As the crowds made their way home from work by the thousands, we greeted them with a smile, a Gospel tract, and the universal language—music. We cranked the sound as loud as it would go and performed Christian music in Portuguese.

As the crowds heard the music, many of them stopped and listened. Some only stopped for a few minutes, while others stayed for the entire concert. At the end, I presented a simple Gospel presentation to several thousand people and gave them an opportunity to speak with a Brazilian Christian.

The entire concert and Gospel presentation lasted about 45 minutes. We took a short break, and as more boats arrived, we started all over again. Literally hundreds became Christ followers after each concert. Michael Tait, formerly of the music group DC Talk, was one of the Liberty students and a featured vocalist. He later told me that this trip was a huge influence in his life.

After one concert, I climbed off the truck to get something to drink, and my two teenage daughters Noel and Nikki met me with a 5-year-old boy clutched in their arms. His name was Nildo. They had been standing in the back with my wife, distributing tracts, when they noticed the little boy. All he had on was a dirty pair of shorts. He had no shoes . . . no shirt . . . no pants.

Noel and Nikki were crying, which immediately got my attention. Through an interpreter, they found out Nildo didn't have a father, and his mother couldn't afford to take care of him. Nildo was living on the streets—taking care of himself. He had no one. He was all alone.

As my girls continued crying, they told me he was hungry, and asked me for money to buy him something to eat. The sight of that homeless little boy had broken their hearts.

Nikki said, "Dad, you see that bench over there? That's where he sleeps, and he told me he takes a shower underneath that drain pipe."

Noel asked, "Do you think we could buy him some clothes?"

I couldn't leave, so I asked one of our missionary friends, Donna Faircloth, if she would be willing to take Noel, Nikki, and Nildo shopping while I started another concert.

Forty-five minutes later, as we finished our second presentation, I looked up the street and saw my daughters and Nildo coming towards me. He wore a bright yellow jogging suit he had picked out himself and a brand new pair of Nike tennis shoes. I could see the smile on his face from two blocks away.

As they came closer, it was evident that Nildo was so excited to be wearing shoes for the first time. Noel told me that when she took him to the bathroom to wash off his feet before putting on the new shoes, his little feet were deformed from roaming the streets barefooted all his life.

Nildo was so excited. He kept saying over and over again in Portuguese, "Shoes, shoes, shoes!"

Noel and Nikki didn't leave his side the whole night. They took turns holding and hugging him as if he were their little brother. At the end of the day, the police were rushing us to move the trailer and bus. We were blocking traffic and everyone was yelling, so we had to pack up and leave quickly.

It all happened so fast we didn't even think about what to do with Nildo, but we knew we couldn't take him with us. The team, my family, and I all got on the bus and left. I still remember watching out the window and seeing that little boy in his bright yellow clothes, waving goodbye. Everyone on the bus was crying.

In the back of the bus was a university student of Japanese descent who had been orphaned and raised by American parents. When he saw Nildo standing there waving as we drove away, he was overcome with emotion and grief. Not a word was spoken as his uncontrollable sobbing was heard all the way to the front of the bus.

On our way back to the hotel, Noel and Nikki pleaded with me to do something to help Nildo. I made some phone calls and found a Christian foster-care home nearby that was willing to take him. The cost was only $400 for an entire year.

Later that evening, I called all of the students together and told them what we could do for Nildo. Then I took off my hat and passed it around. It was the end of the trip and all they had left was a little money for snacks and souvenirs.

While we were literally "passing the hat," a Brazilian pastor traveling with us leaned over to me and said, "Don't you know that there are thousands of homeless children on the streets of Brazil? There is no way you can help them all."

I knew he was well-meaning, but I believe it was then God taught me an important lesson—one that has guided my life ever since. The pastor was right . . . we couldn't help them all, but we could help one little boy—we could help Nildo.

I reminded him of the words of Jesus, *"Whatever you did for one of the least of these brothers of mine, you did for me."*[7]

That night, in a real sense, we passed the hat for Jesus.

I was shocked when we counted the money—over $800, enough to provide two years of foster care for Nildo.

We were all so excited as we returned to the boat docks the

next day. As soon as we arrived, Noel and Nikki looked around excitedly for Nildo to give him the wonderful news. But they couldn't find him.

They searched and searched where he had been the day before, but he was nowhere to be found. Finally, after nearly an hour, they found him several blocks away. He was bloody, bruised, and lying in the corner of an abandoned building.

The older street children had beaten him, taking his new clothes and shoes. All he had left was his dirty pair of torn shorts.

I'll never forget the look on my girls' faces as they carried this broken little boy in their arms back to the boat docks.

Nikki asked, "Dad, can we buy him some more new clothes?"

"Of course," I said, "just don't get bright yellow this time."

Off they went again and returned with another jogging suit. This time it was gray and they bought an identical pair of Nike tennis shoes.

Noel and Nikki asked Nildo if he wanted to get off the streets and live in a Christian children's home. He immediately said, "Yes!"

That night, when it was time to leave, Nildo was with us on the bus.

When we arrived at the hotel, Nikki said, "Dad, Nildo needs to take a shower, but he won't take off his new shoes. Will you help me?"

I tried for 30 minutes with an interpreter to explain he only had to take them off for five minutes while taking a shower, and then he could put them back on again. But he wouldn't budge! I finally talked him into taking them off while I stood right outside the shower stall, holding his tennis shoes so he could see them while he took his shower.

As soon as he dried off, he put the shoes right back on—he

even slept in them.

That night, as I tucked that little 5-year-old boy into bed and prayed with him, I told him he was going to have a new mom and dad soon. The next morning, I put my arms around Noel and Nikki and said, "If you never do another kind deed in your lives, you have done something wonderful for this little boy."

That next year, we thought about Nildo often. Noel and Nikki kept in touch, and we received reports that he was doing well in school, attending church, and had even become a Christ follower.

That summer, I took another group of students back to Brazil, but this time my family couldn't join me. As I walked out the door, Nikki hugged me and said, "Dad, will you try to see Nildo? And when you find him, will you give him this picture of our family and buy him some new shoes?" How could I refuse? I was excited to see Nildo again.

When I got to Brazil, I was on a mission. I even did something that I hate to do—I went shopping. I bought shoes, a backpack, school supplies, soccer balls—I went just a little overboard.

But I wasn't ready for what I saw. Nildo came to the hotel where we were staying to have dinner—I almost didn't recognize him. He was so well-dressed and well-mannered.

He said to me in perfect English, "Hello, Mr. Brewer, how are Nikki and Noel?"

I hugged him and gave him the family photo they had placed in a plastic frame. He hugged and kissed it and started telling everyone around him in loud Portuguese, "These are my American sisters! They took me off the streets." It wasn't long before we were all crying again, but this time they were tears of joy.

I also gave him a Bible my family had signed as a keepsake.

A few months later on Christmas Eve, we were sitting in the family room when the phone rang. It was Donna from Brazil, who had helped Noel and Nikki buy the clothes for Nildo. She said, "Someone wants to talk to you." Nildo picked up the phone and wished us a Merry Christmas and Happy New Year. That was about all he could say in English. When Donna returned to the line, she said, "You're not going to believe what happened yesterday. I am in Rio for Christmas and was visiting the church where we have partnered for the past two summers. The pastor recognized me in the audience and asked me to come to the platform to give a word of greeting.

"While I was speaking, I heard a loud commotion in the balcony and looked up just in time to see a little boy jump from the balcony to the platform. He was yelling in Portuguese, 'Aunty! Aunty! Aunty!' It was Nildo. He didn't know I was going to be there that day, and I didn't expect to see him either. When he saw me, he was just so excited! And you won't believe what he had with him. When I reached down to hug him, he was holding a plastic frame with your family's picture and the Bible you all signed. He must take them with him everywhere he goes!"

In 1996, World Help began its Child Sponsorship Program with the help of my daughter Noel, who was inspired by a very special little boy. She remembered the words of that well-meaning pastor, "There is no way you can help them all." But she also remembered Nildo and the difference that can be made in one life.

Because of Nildo, World Help has found sponsors for thousands of children in need.

Nildo is now a grown young man. He continues to serve Christ and has finished school. I am so proud of him.

When I think of Nildo today, I can only imagine what his life might have been like had he not met Noel and Nikki that day. God had a plan for his life just like He has a plan for my life and your life. Nildo is a living reminder that we can change the world—one child at a time.

CHAPTER SIX

there lies the dead god of communism

"MY SOUL THIRSTS FOR GOD, FOR THE LIVING GOD. WHEN CAN I GO AND MEET WITH GOD?"

—PSALM 42:2

O n a cold November night, we stood in the snow at Red Square and worshipped God—Red Square, the same place where tanks rolled and the Red Army paraded in front of Lenin, Stalin, and Khrushchev. We were there and the world was changing right before our eyes.

This was my first visit to Russia and the Cold War was coming to a close. Gorbachev slowly introduced Glasnost and Perestroika to the Russian people. It was a memorable and surreal experience. Since then, I have returned to Moscow more than 40 times and taken thousands of Americans to see what they never dreamed would be possible in their lifetime.

I remember waking the morning after our visit to Red Square, anticipating what God had in store for us. Our small group carried in hundreds of Russian Bibles in our suitcases, wondering how we would distribute them. I took about 10 copies and stuffed them into my coat pockets.

That morning, we stood in a long line to visit Lenin's tomb in the middle of Red Square. One of the Liberty University students who was traveling with me said, "I didn't know John Lennon was buried in Moscow."

I just shook my head and said, "That would be Vladimir

Lenin, thank you very much."

Suddenly, the line stopped moving. We found ourselves standing directly in front of the eternal flame, a monument to Russia's Unknown Soldier.

It was Saturday morning, the day when many weddings take place in Russia. I soon discovered it's a Russian tradition for young married couples to visit the eternal flame after their civil ceremony to pay their respects.

While we stood there, one young Russian couple after another in wedding attire stood at the eternal flame for a moment of silence and had their photograph taken. When I realized what was happening, I impulsively got out of line and walked up to one couple. "*Podarok*," I said, which is Russian for "gift." I gave that young couple their first wedding gift—a copy of a Russian Bible.

I repeated this until my 10 Bibles were gone. Some of the couples thanked me, "*Spasibo . . . Bol'shoe spasibo*" or "Thank you . . . thank you, very much." Some of them kissed their new Bibles. One couple proudly held their Bible up while the photographer shot their wedding photo.

Once my Bibles were gone, I returned to the line as it started moving again. When we reached the mausoleum of Lenin, the soldiers made us take off our hats and coats. They told us to take our hands out of our pockets and sternly commanded us to stop talking—not even a whisper. As we filed by the mummified body of Vladimir Lenin, lying in state in a glass coffin, it dawned on me what those soldiers were doing. They were forcing us to be respectful. They wanted us to pay our respects to their "god."

When we walked out of the tomb, I remarked to my friends, "There lies the dead god of communism!"

That evening we still didn't know how we would distribute the remainder of the Bibles, but we wanted to make sure every copy got in just the right hands.

The next day, we visited the only Protestant church at that time in all of Moscow, a city of nine million people. My friend Peter Deyneka, who is now in heaven, asked me to preach while he interpreted. It was a privilege. When I was finished, several people came forward seeking Christ, including a Russian soldier in uniform. Many were baptized that night.

Much to my surprise, a group of pastors were in the service that night from all over Russia, some as far away as Siberia. They were in Moscow for a week of intensive leadership training. It was an honor to meet with them after the service, to hear their stories of what God was doing, to pray with them, encourage them, and give each of them a stack of Russian Bibles to take home on the train the next day.

There I was in a communist country—an atheist country—but we had distributed 500 Bibles that would be spread throughout all of Russia.

CHAPTER SEVEN

you are the first americans
to keep your promise

"GOD HAS GIVEN US TWO HANDS, ONE TO RECEIVE WITH AND THE OTHER TO GIVE WITH."

—BILLY GRAHAM[8]

I t was in the early months of the fall of communism; everywhere I turned I saw poverty, broken infrastructure, and lots of pot holes in the roads. The majority of Russian men were drunk on Vodka by noon. They had nothing to live for and no hope for the future. All I saw were blank looks on people's faces. The streets were dark, there were long lines for food, and all too often, the stores ran out of supplies before 10 a.m. Those were depressing times.

Because we were Americans with the name "World Help," I was invited to visit Cancer Hospital #62, the leading cancer institute in all of Russia. At first, I didn't want to go. As a cancer survivor, the thought of seeing terminally ill patients in a hopeless situation was traumatic for me. My Russian host and interpreter said, "You must go. They are expecting you." Reluctantly, I agreed to the visit, but I wasn't looking forward to it.

When I got there, much to my surprise, more than 300 people were waiting in the large meeting room to greet me. It was crowded with doctors and nurses in long white gowns, some patients in wheel chairs, and others with walkers. Some were even rolled in on their beds. The only two patients in the entire hospital who were not there were in intensive care.

I looked around at all the suffering cancer patients—waiting to die. They were not dying from cancer alone but from lack of adequate medical treatment they desperately needed. As a cancer survivor, this was almost too much to bear, too much to see.

I remembered I had several boxes of Russian New Testaments in the vehicle outside. We gave each patient one as a gift—they were all so excited.

Although it was difficult for me to be there that day, I could easily relate to the patients' suffering. I knew the pain they were feeling, and I understood the fear in their eyes. Hospital officials asked me to speak to the patients and share my faith.

I began by saying, "I am a cancer survivor." Immediately, many people in the room began to weep.

Then I realized there were probably very few cancer survivors at that time in Moscow. Basically, they were sent to this hospital to die. Even though these patients were in a top Russian medical facility with wonderful doctors and nurses, their medical resources were almost non-existent. They had very little pain medication or chemotherapy; they didn't even have enough rubber gloves. The hospital paid two people each night to wash the gloves used that day so doctors and nurses could reuse them again in the morning.

I looked into the faces of men and women who would be dead in a few months. It was extremely painful.

"Yes, I am a cancer survivor," I told them, "but someday I will die, and so will you. Today, I have come to tell you how you can live forever."

For the next 15 minutes, I shared my faith through an interpreter. More than 50 of the doctors, nurses, and patients came to faith in Jesus Christ that day in Cancer Hospital #62.

After I spoke, hospital staff members took me on a tour of

the hospital. This was a very emotional experience. I saw empty medicine cabinets and patients in recovery with no bandages to cover their wounds. Shocked, I witnessed a patient who had just received a tracheotomy and because no surgical tubing was available, the doctors placed a used soda straw in his throat so he could breathe.

My first response was to turn and run from this frightening sight, but I knew God sent me to that hospital for a reason—to help these people.

Dr. Mahkson, the chief surgeon of the hospital, gave me a list of urgent needs—several pages long. He asked for my help. I looked at the list and immediately said, "I can't promise you how much I will be able to help, but I will promise you this . . . I will help you."

Several weeks later, on my next visit to Moscow, I led a team with Joni Eareckson Tada and 66 of her friends. Many of them were physically disabled and in wheelchairs. We spent the entire week visiting hospitals, orphanages, and public schools, distributing New Testaments. Joni presented her powerful testimony of overcoming suffering and finding the hope in life.

Friday evening in the Olympic village, several thousand people packed in to hear her, and hundreds came to faith in Christ. On Monday night at dinner, one of Joni's friends rolled over to my table in his wheelchair and told me he had a friend in Tucson, Arizona, who had a warehouse full of medical supplies— just collecting dust.

"If I can get him to donate these to World Help," he asked me, "will you see that they get to Cancer Hospital #62?" I immediately agreed, and he was thrilled.

When he wheeled back to his table, I turned to my Russian host and asked him what it would cost to ship a container of medical supplies from the U.S. to Moscow. He said it would cost at least $10,000.

My first thought was, "Dear God, what have I done?" But I quickly reminded myself that the same God who healed me from cancer was in control of this situation too. Little did I realize how much in control He was.

A few hours later, I attended the world famous Bolshoi Ballet with Joni and her friends. I wasn't thrilled to be there. My idea of fun is watching 22 men in pads and helmets pounding their opponents, not watching men tiptoe around in white tights pretending to be swans—no offense to people who like swans and the ballet.

I woke up at half time, which I'm told they call "intermission." Much to my surprise, I recognized two U.S. Congressmen standing in the aisle, Congressman Newt Gingrich of Georgia and Congressman Dick Gephardt of Missouri. The Republican was standing on the right and the Democrat on the left—I couldn't help but find that amusing.

Being the bashful soul that I am, I introduced myself to them. They asked me why I was in Moscow, and I told them about Joni and her friends and all the wonderful things God had done that week. They were genuinely interested. Then I asked them what they were doing there. They said, "We are here to finalize the details of the Russian American Aid Package."

I remember thinking, "Hmmm . . . Russian American Aid Package . . . Hmmm."

My brain shifted into high gear. "Congressmen," I said, "if I had a container of medical supplies that needed to be shipped from the U.S. to Cancer Hospital #62 in Moscow, could that be considered part of the Russian American Aid Package?"

They both replied, "Yes, of course!" God was obviously working behind the scenes to fulfill His plan.

The Congressmen gave me the name of their liaison, and

when I returned to the U.S., we immediately went to work. Louanne Guillerman, whose husband was then president of Liberty University, volunteered to travel to Tucson to inventory the medical supplies and ship them to our offices in Virginia.

It was a happy, memorable day when the National Guard came to our office, inspected the container, sealed it, and officially made it part of the Russian American Aid Package. That first container was shipped, at no cost to World Help, to Cancer Hospital #62 in Moscow, Russia—our tax dollars at work.

I couldn't be in Moscow when the container arrived, but I sent my oldest daughter Noel to represent me. I'll never forget watching the news on CNN as Boris Yeltsin stood on a tank and the Russian White House was bombed during the early days of Russia's democracy. Knowing my daughter was staying just blocks away, I prayed that she would be safe.

When the World Help container arrived at the hospital, the doctors and nurses lined up in front of the building. Noel later told me, "Dad, you wouldn't have believed it. While we were unloading the boxes, one of the surgeons ran out of the operating room, ripped open a box and grabbed a package of surgical tubing and said, 'I need this right now!' and then immediately went back inside and saved someone's life.

"And," she said, "Dr. Mahkson put his hands on my shoulders and said, 'Young lady, please give your father a message from me. Please tell him I said thank you for all of this help. And please, please tell him you are the first Americans to keep your promise to us.'"

Before we started helping Cancer Hospital #62, they had not received any outside help. Since that day, we have shipped 13 containers to them with medical supplies valued at nearly $2 million dollars.

A few years later, one of our World Help Russian staff

members was diagnosed with cancer. Because of the relationship we had built with the cancer hospital, she was able to become a patient and receive the care she needed. One of the nurses even told her that the gurney she was lying on and many of the supplies used to treat her were donated through World Help. She is now a cancer survivor.

On one of my last visits to the hospital, Dr. Mahkson took me aside and said, "At first, I did not believe in your faith. But I have seen it in action and now I accept your faith."

God opened the door, World Help walked through it, and hundreds have not only been treated and cured of cancer, but they accepted Jesus Christ. They are true survivors—they will live forever!

CHAPTER EIGHT

you are sitting in the room where communism began

"THEN YOU WILL KNOW THE TRUTH, AND THE TRUTH WILL SET YOU FREE."

—JOHN 8:32

Sasha Semchenko spent three years in a Russian prison. His only crime was distributing copies of the Gospel of John at the Moscow airport.

Sasha was introduced to me shortly after World Help became involved in distributing Bibles in Russia, and we became good friends and partners in ministry.

One evening while I was having dinner in his apartment, he introduced me to his five daughters. They were dressed beautifully in their smocked Russian dresses. One by one, he called their names. When he got to his youngest, he said, "She is my favorite."

I thought this was rather unusual for him to say, especially in front of her four sisters. Then he added, "She was born while I was in prison. She was nearly three years old before she saw her Papa for the first time." Then I understood why she meant so much to him.

Sasha was owner of a Protestant publishing company, the only one of its kind in those early days after the Soviet Union was dismantled. He was well-connected. He had friends in the Russian parliament and owned a construction company with hundreds of employees.

One evening, not long after the new Russian Republic had begun, Sasha scheduled a dinner at a restaurant for me and our team to meet some of his friends. Our small group consisted of three World Help board members: Dan Reber, Jimmy Thomas, and Earl Clarkson, and my interpreter, a student at Moscow State University.

We were already seated when Sasha and his friends arrived. He brought with him the vice president of Russia and his wife, and the head of the former KGB and his wife. The men were well-dressed in suits and ties, and the women wore mink stoles. Here we were in our jeans, tennis shoes, and polo shirts. We had worked hard that day and were just expecting to have a nice, leisurely dinner with some of Sasha's old friends. Sasha forgot to tell us who he was bringing with him.

When my young interpreter saw the vice president walk in, he almost went into cardiac arrest. "Please don't make me interpret tonight," he said. But he was the only one there who could do it, and he finally calmed down.

After the awkwardness of our initial shock and lack of proper attire, we enjoyed a wonderful dinner. I told Sasha's friends about our desire and plans to help Russia. The vice president stood and made a toast—typically Russian. "Thank you for coming, thank you for your help," he said. "The only solution for my country is not a political solution but a spiritual solution."

I truly believe he meant every word.

On my next visit to Russia, Sasha arranged a meeting for me with government officials inside the Kremlin. The new Russian Parliament was debating whether or not to allow Protestants to have religious freedom. The outcome was seriously in doubt.

Our American delegation included my good friend Jay Strack, vice president of the Southern Baptist Convention at that time, and lifelong friends Roger and Bill Breland. It was one of those "pinch me" experiences . . . we were inside the Kremlin, meeting with President Boris Yeltsin's chief of staff and several members of his Cabinet. They were cordial and listened while we pled our case.

At the conclusion of our meeting, the chief of staff said, "It is interesting you would sit here and talk about religious freedom in this room."

"Why?" I asked.

"This room was Vladimir Lenin's office," he said. "You are sitting in the room where communism began."

CHAPTER NINE

i don't believe in jesus christ

"HE WHO HAS THE SON HAS LIFE; HE WHO DOES
NOT HAVE THE SON OF GOD DOES NOT HAVE LIFE."

—I JOHN 5:12

F
or decades, Russians were taught there was no God. Of course, many didn't believe that, but atheism was still the official religious position of the country.

Because I traveled quietly for years (under the radar) into Eastern Europe prior to the fall of communism, I established many close and valued friendships. So when the Berlin Wall came down, and the historic opportunity to plant the seeds of the Gospel in Russia opened up, I wasted no time. I was one of the first to walk through that open door.

I had the publishing rights for a Russian/English parallel New Testament—with the Russian text in one column and the corresponding English text next to it. I had no idea how God would use this tool and how popular it would be.

During one of my earlier visits to Moscow, I met with the minister of defense and several of his generals and their wives. We had dinner at a Russian restaurant. I still remember the taste of caviar . . . yuck! I like my eggs over easy.

I took a copy of this special edition New Testament with me, and I remember gathering enough nerve to ask for permission to distribute the books on Russian military bases. I was prepared to argue my case, but much to my surprise, the officials immediately said, "Yes," and asked me for an initial order of 500,000 copies.

Years before, Stalin ordered his men to burn many churches and Bibles, so there were very few copies available anywhere.

When the wife of the minister of defense opened the book and saw it was in both Russian and English, her face lit up. She slipped the New Testament into her purse and never gave it back. That was my first indication we had struck a nerve.

The Russian people were hungry for the Word of God but also eager to learn English. Not only did the Russian military give us permission to distribute these rare books; officials also allowed us unprecedented access to distribute them on the military bases.

World Help's vocal group *MISSION* was with me on this particular trip, and at the first military base we visited, the commander met us at the front gate. His orders allowed us on the base to not only distribute these New Testaments, but to share our faith with the soldiers publicly and privately. The first words out of his mouth were not, "Welcome. How are you?" Instead, in typical Russian fashion, he got straight to the point, "I want you to know—I don't believe in Jesus Christ."

While our team unloaded boxes of New Testaments from the bus, I struck up a conversation with the commander. I asked him to tell me a little about himself. Eventually, he mentioned his 14-year-old daughter.

"Ah," he said, "she believes in Jesus Christ. One day, someone gave her a Bible and she brought it home and began reading it every day. Not long afterwards she announced, 'Papa, I believe in Jesus Christ.'"

There it was—my open door. For nearly an hour, I shared my faith and what it means to follow Christ. He listened respectfully to what I had to say. He was so close—but not ready.

I have thought of that day often, wondering what kept him from making the choice right then. Perhaps it was because he was surrounded by his men or that we had just met and I was an American. Whatever the reason, he was reluctant.

He did promise to read the Russian/English New Testament I gave him, and then, unexpectedly, he allowed me to pray for him. I asked God to allow his 14-year-old daughter to be the one to show him the way.

That was a remarkable day. We distributed hundreds of copies of God's Word, many Russian soldiers placed their faith in Jesus, and a Russian commander heard the good news of the death, burial and resurrection of Christ.

Occasionally, I think about the commander and wonder if I will see him in heaven.

CHAPTER TEN

we want you to give the graduation address

"I DIDN'T COME HERE TO SIT SILENTLY WITH MY HANDS FOLDED ON MY LAP. I CAME TO SPEAK ABOUT CHRIST."

—PRISONER FOR CHRIST IN RUSSIA

I was met at the door by the school principal, a rather large Russian woman who towered over me. I was a little intimidated but was also struck by her opening words of greeting. She bent down and whispered in my ear, "I believe in Jesus Christ."

For a second, I thought back to the day before on the military base. The commander's first words were, "I don't believe in Jesus Christ." What a contrast.

When we arrived at this public school in Moscow, arrangements had been made for us to give all 300 students a copy of the Russian/English New Testament. The Russian minister of education had already seen a copy and had given permission for it to be used as an English textbook in the public schools.

The economy in Russia was nearly bankrupt. Years of communism left many Russians below the poverty level, and the schools were in dire need of textbooks.

The principal invited me into her office. In a hushed voice, she shared her faith in Jesus Christ, thanked me for the textbooks, and asked me to give an English lesson from them to the entire school. Then, with a wink and nod, she said, "Of course, you must also share the Gospel."

I'm sure it wasn't my brilliant attempt at an English lesson, but it was one of those magic moments when 300 students were quiet and attentive—it astounded me. I shared my faith and what it means to be a Christ follower as they held their new English textbooks—Russian/English New Testaments. It was truly a "God moment."

That day, many of those students determined to follow Christ and a new revolution began in Russia.

We were able to visit another high school in Moscow and as soon as we arrived, we noticed something different—something was going on. Instead of the jeans and t-shirts most Russian students wore to school, the guys were dressed in coats and ties, and girls were wearing long dresses. There were balloons everywhere and a table in the back with Russian cakes and punch. Many parents were arriving. I thought to myself, "Wow! How did they know we were coming? News sure travels fast."

We made our way to the principal's office, obviously delighted that we would be accepted so graciously.

We soon discovered the celebration wasn't for us after all; it was their graduation day.

I immediately apologized and offered to come back another time. The principal wouldn't hear of it. He asked us to stay, and asked *MISSION* to be the special entertainment for the ceremony. Then he turned to me and said, "We want you to give the graduation address. Do you have anything you could say?"

Me . . . have anything to say?

In politically correct America, we cannot even mention God in a high school graduation ceremony. But that day, in a Russian public school, we presented hundreds of copies of the New Testament to every student, faculty member, and parent. *MISSION* shared their faith through song, and I gave a clear presentation of the Gospel. I wondered which country had the most religious freedom.

At the close of the ceremony, many of the students and faculty stood to their feet and publicly placed their faith in Jesus Christ.

The English teacher came up to me afterward and introduced herself. She thanked me for the gifts, and said she would begin using the New Testaments to teach English immediately.

Then she smiled and said, "Today, I too became a believer. Every day we are required to begin class by standing and reciting these words: 'Lenin lived, Lenin lives, Lenin will live forever.' Beginning tomorrow," she said, "I am going to begin every class with prayer. Thank you for making this such a special day."

In the days that followed, we distributed more than 500,000 New Testaments on military bases and in the public schools, and millions of copies of the Gospel were distributed to nearly every home and apartment in Moscow.

CHAPTER ELEVEN

the concert has been cancelled

"THE KING'S HEART IS IN THE HAND OF THE LORD, LIKE THE RIVERS OF WATER HE TURNS IT WHEREVER HE WISHES."

—PROVERBS 21:1, NKJV

"I am sorry, but the concert has been cancelled" were the first words I heard from the commanding officer as I stepped off our bus at the gate of a Russian military base. The leadership had never allowed a group of foreigners on that base before, especially Americans.

"Why?" I asked the commander.

"There are no soldiers here," he said. "They are all out in the field doing military maneuvers."

I suspected he had "gotten wind" about us and what we planned to do, and he was not thrilled. After all, he was a general in the Russian army, a Communist—an atheist.

I told him we had permission from the minister of defense, but he was not impressed. He turned to walk away, and I immediately grabbed my interpreter by the arm and followed him.

I think he was a little shocked that I wouldn't leave. He repeated several times, "I am sorry, but the concert has been cancelled. There are no soldiers here." While he spoke these words, a truckload of men drove past us. I said, "What about them? Can't we do a concert for them?"

"*Nyet*," he would say, "*Nyet. Nyet. Nyet!*" I could tell I was on the verge of making him angry—something I didn't want to do—so I went into begging mode.

"I have a busload of Americans over there that have paid their way to come to Russia," I said. "They told all their friends back home we would be able to present a concert on this military base and distribute New Testaments to the soldiers. Now you're telling me we must go home and tell our friends the concert was cancelled. It will be such an embarrassment," I said. "Please don't allow us to be humiliated like this!"

I was either very convincing or else he just wanted to get rid of me. Either way, it worked.

"All right," he said. "You can do your concert, but only for a few men."

We unloaded the bus quickly and set up our equipment in record time. All of the commotion, which may have been "accidentally" louder than normal, let everyone know there was a group of Americans on the base. Word spread quickly. In an unbelievable turn of events, as we were setting up for the concert for only a handful of soldiers, a convoy of trucks returned to the military base from field maneuvers.

By the time the concert began, the auditorium was packed with more than 400 uniformed soldiers. A huge statue of Vladimir Lenin was on the stage and a giant mural depicting the virtues of communism was on the back wall. This was one of Moscow's most strategic military bases, and I was positive this was the first time the Gospel was ever proclaimed from that stage. God miraculously brought those men back to base that night . . . and sitting right in the middle of the front row was their commander.

That evening, we gave our gifts of New Testaments to all the soldiers. *MISSION* shared through their music, and I preached the death, burial, and resurrection with newfound freedom and boldness.

Two things happened that night that I will always remember. First, more than 40 Russian soldiers stood to their feet and publicly prayed to receive Jesus Christ, including the commander. Second, after being with us for an entire week and translating the Gospel from English to Russian many, many times, my interpreter also became a believer. She and her family have become dear friends, and every time I return to Moscow, I visit them. We always talk about that night when the concert was cancelled.

CHAPTER TWELVE

moscow for jesus

"EARLY THAT SUNDAY MORNING, FATHER ALEXANDER MENN CLOSES THE FRONT DOOR SOFTLY BEHIND HIM, NOT TO WAKEN HIS WIFE, AND PASSES THROUGH THE GATE IN THE STOCKADE FENCE. WALKING BRISKLY, HE CROSSES THE STREET TO A WOODLAND PATH THAT LEADS TO THE VILLAGE. THE SUN IS BARELY ABOVE THE HORIZON AND THE WOODS ARE SHADOWED AND COLD.

HE HAS FOLLOWED THIS ROUTINE FOR A THOUSAND SUNDAYS: THE SEVEN-MINUTE WALK TO THE TRAIN STATION TO CATCH THE 6:50 LOCAL TO MOSCOW; GETTING OFF AT PUSHKINO, THE MARKET TOWN, TO BOARD THE NO. 24 BUS TO HIS PARISH CHURCH IN THE VILLAGE OF NOVAYA DEREVNYA; ARRIVING IN GOOD TIME FOR THE 8 A.M. SERVICE.

BUT NOT TODAY. TODAY—SEPTEMBER 9, 1990—HIS PARISHIONERS WILL WAIT IN VAIN."

—LAWRENCE ELLIOTT[9]

Alexander Menn, 55, was a rather robust man with a thick salt and pepper beard. He was an emerging spiritual leader of the Russian Orthodox Church. Keeping his independence through the Brezhnev years, Menn refused to cooperate with the KGB and endured harassment, interrogations, and threats.

He never faltered in his stand on religious brotherhood and tolerance and spoke on reform, redemption, and self-determination. Menn was an honest, uncompromising man who offered God's consolation to unbearably hard and empty lives. He loved Jesus Christ, the Russian people, the Russian language, and the Russian culture, and he expressed the Gospel in a way that people loved to hear it. He was well-known and well-loved throughout the U.S.S.R.

Because of that, Menn was the focus of fear, loathing, and eventually, murder.

Although police cling to the theory that robbery was the motive, evidence points to a different scenario. The blade of an ax was driven into the base of his skull from behind. Murder, not robbery, was the objective. The ax, a horrifying historic symbol of revenge, was also the murder weapon used when Stalin ordered Leon Trotsky eliminated half a century ago. The stricken Menn didn't die instantly, but staggered toward home and collapsed in a crumpled heap by the fence to his yard. That is where his wife found him—he had bled to death.

To this day, there has been no final investigation into Menn's death. Some believe this is because he died at the hands of the KGB. His crime: the winning of so many new believers who turned their backs on the one creed the state sanctioned—communism.

His killer must now realize what history attests: to create a Christian martyr is to guarantee his work will endure.

Whatever the true facts of his death, Menn had a burning desire to see his countrymen converted. Even though he is gone, Menn's burden for his people survived and lives on in a special book he wrote right before his death, *To Be a Christian*. In the words of an old Russian proverb, "What is written with a pen cannot be hacked away even by an ax."

To Be a Christian answers, explains, discusses, and defends the Gospel of Jesus Christ in the language, history, and culture of the Russian people. Because it was written by a fellow Russian, it answers their most important questions: How do you know God exists? Why become a Christian? Why does God allow evil? What is the difference between Christianity and other religions? The book explains the sinless life of Jesus and His death, burial, and resurrection. It also explains the "Christian life," gives a detailed plan of salvation, and ends with an invitation for the reader to personally receive Christ as Savior.

Because Russians deserve to hear the Gospel in their own language and culture, World Help began the monumental task of providing a copy of *To Be a Christian* to every home in Moscow. That calculated to three million homes.

The Russian people are highly educated and love to read, but they were raised for two generations under atheism. They have no foundation of belief in God. With the collapse of communism, there exists a spiritual vacuum, and the door is wide open for either the Gospel of Jesus Christ or man-made religions and cults.

Because of the Russians' long history of atheism, they needed more than God's Word; they needed a clear, more exhaustive explanation of the Gospel. They needed the most basic concept: "How to Know God Exists."

To Be a Christian was the "miracle" we needed to help reach the Russian people with the Gospel, and the "Moscow for Jesus" campaign became the vehicle for reaching Moscow.

Our carefully planned mission included a massive mailing campaign reaching every home in the city of Moscow, a comprehensive pastoral training conference, Bible distribution, humanitarian relief, preaching engagements, and finally, a city-wide crusade in Moscow's Olympic Stadium.

Three million copies of *To Be a Christian* were printed on former communist-owned presses and distributed to the city's 11 million residents, which included 500,000 university students.

Our pastors' conference marked the first occasion in which Russian and American pastors ministered side by side. Nearly 400 Russian pastors and 16 American pastors met for this historic gathering. Attendees arrived from throughout the former Soviet Union, some traveling for several days just to get to the conference.

For more than 70 years, it was illegal for Russian pastors to meet. But now that there was religious freedom, most could not afford the expense of a trip to Moscow. World Help paid for the Russian pastors' travel expenses, meals, and lodging, making it possible for them to attend.

Each pastor received a 186-page notebook with the outlines of each session translated into Russian. After each session and during every break, the Russian pastors crowded around the Americans and engaged in spirited question-and-answer sessions—they were hungry to learn. The pastors had no libraries to speak of, so World Help presented each pastor with more than 200 Christian books, Bibles, and commentaries.

With tears in his eyes, one Russian pastor said, "I have been praying for a concordance for over two years, and now I finally have one."

They also received copies of the Russian version of *The JESUS Film*. More than six billion people have seen the film in over 200 countries, and more than 200 million people have indicated decisions to follow Christ after watching the film. [10]

According to the U.S. Center for World Missions, "No single evangelistic campaign in human history has touched as many lives as the showing of this film worldwide."[11]

We also conducted a city-wide evangelistic program. Five teams of American pastors and church leaders penetrated the 100 square miles of Moscow, and distributed more than 200,000 Bibles and Christian books in evangelistic services. They gave more than $60,000 worth of basic medical supplies to hospitals that were hard-pressed to find even aspirin or band-aids.

The teams encountered communities that had never heard an American speaker, churches that had never hosted any foreign visitor, and orphanages and schools that had never heard the Gospel.

Finally, more than 10,000 people attended the campaign's closing rally at Olympic Stadium. The rally featured a musical drama with a huge cast of actors and an original score. A 10-minute video depicted one of Alexander Menn's last sermons, including biblical scenes and illustrations. Everyone who attended the gathering received a Russian New Testament and a copy of Menn's 320-page book, *The Son of Man*, a chronicle of the life of Christ.

Nearly 5,000 people stood at the close of the service to accept Christ as their Savior. We had a total of 7,756 recorded decisions in 10 days.

It was a new day in Russia. The doors of freedom had swung wide open and the Word of God came flooding in.

CHAPTER THIRTEEN

35 da ma zhan

"THERE ARE CHRISTIANS AROUND THE WORLD TODAY WHO ARE LIVING UNDER TERROR AND ARE NOT INTIMIDATED INTO BEING 'TOLERANT' AND COMPROMISING THEIR FAITH. THESE BELIEVERS IN RESTRICTED NATIONS GO ABOUT THE BUSINESS OF LIFE MORE FOCUSED ON THE ETERNAL THINGS THAT DO NOT CHANGE. THESE SHINING LIGHTS ON A HILL TEACH US TO LOVE OUR ENEMIES BY LIFTING UP CHRIST IN EXTRAORDINARY CIRCUMSTANCES."

—TOM WHITE[12]

A s I stepped into the taxi, I pulled a crumpled sheet of paper out of my pocket. On it was written an address in both English and Cantonese: 35 Da Ma Zhan.

In Guangzhou, a city of over three million people, I was alone and had no idea where I was going. My goal was to meet one of China's most well-known house church leaders, Lin Xiangao, who also used the Western name, Samuel Lamb.

When the Chinese taxi driver stopped in the middle of the street, I said, "No, no," and once again pointed to the small sheet of paper. He nodded yes and pointed me in the direction of a small alley, barely 20 feet wide. "Da Ma Zhan," he said. It was nearly dark outside and the alley was packed with people. Families sat outside their doorways, mothers cooked rice, and older men—wearing their blue Mao jackets—played Mah-Jongg, a Chinese game that looked a lot like Dominos to me. The smells of fish, steamed rice, and vegetables filled the air. I felt I had stepped back in time.

Walking down the alley, I felt a little intimidated, but I had come too far to let fear stop me. I arrived at number 35—a small three-story apartment building—and as I expected, uniformed armed guards met me. They occupied the first floor, guarding Pastor Lamb who was under house arrest. He has endured more than 21 years in prison for his faith and because he would not register his church with the Chinese government. Fifteen of those years, he did hard physical labor in a coal mine after he tried to make a copy of the New Testament.

While Pastor Lamb was in prison, his wife died, but the authorities never bothered to give him the news. Eleven months later, his mother—who was also living in their home—passed away. After his eventual release, he returned to his apartment and learned of their deaths.

I was eager to meet Pastor Lamb. His house church meeting had just dismissed, so I had to wait outside while hundreds of Chinese believers made their way down the narrow staircase and filed past me into the night. I had to push past the guards to make my way up the stairs. When I reached the third floor, I met my hero for the first time.

Pastor Lamb was short—I towered over him. With a contagious smile, he invited me to come in. The first thing I remember seeing was a long table with about 20 Chinese young people writing feverishly. Nearly 80 percent of the pastor's congregation is young people who are hungry for the Word of God and eager to share it with their friends.

I asked Pastor Lamb what they were doing. He matter-of-factly explained, "They are making handwritten copies of the Gospel of John to give to their friends at school tomorrow. We only have one Bible at this time, so we must make copies."

I thought to myself, "This would never happen in my country. Most Christian young people in America would never think of giving a Gospel of John to their friends in school, let alone make a handwritten copy."

As I sat there with this leader of the house church movement, he told me his stories and showed me his photos and an official Oval Office pen from Ronald Reagan. It was a gift from a White House staff member who told him, "President Reagan told me to ask you to pray for him whenever you use this pen."

He showed me a photo of Billy Graham standing behind the makeshift pulpit in that Da Ma Zhan apartment. As I looked around the apartment, I noticed the walls had been knocked out and replaced with wooden benches. In the far corner was a single bed, a small refrigerator, and a hot plate—Pastor Lamb's living space. Every single inch of the rest of the apartment was converted to a meeting room for the Da Ma Zhan Church.

Pastor Lamb said he started preaching again when he was released from prison, and his house church started growing. One day, concerned authorities stormed into the meeting and arrested Pastor Lamb again. They confiscated all the Bibles and hymnals. For three days, he was interrogated, beaten, and tortured. He was told to go back and close the Da Ma Zhan house church. I asked him, "What did you do?"

"I stood in the church the next week," he said, "and told the congregation that the police said not to come back."

"What happened?" I asked.

"The next Sunday," he said, "our church attendance doubled. Jesus said, '*Upon this rock I will build my church; and the gates of hell shall not prevail against it.'"*[13]

At the time, Da Ma Zhan Church was one of the largest house churches in China. Every week, more than 1,500 believers packed into five services.

I asked Pastor Lamb, "How did you survive all those years in prison?"

"I quoted Scripture I had committed to memory and composed hymns to worship God," he said. His two favorite biblical passages were written from prison to the Christians at Philippi and to young Timothy:

> *"Do not be anxious about anything, but in everything, by prayer and petition, with thanksgiving, present your requests to God. And the peace of God, which transcends all understanding, will guard your hearts and your minds in Christ Jesus" (Philippians 4:6-7).*

> *"I have fought the good fight, I have finished the race, I have kept the faith. Now there is in store for me the crown of righteousness, which the Lord, the righteous Judge, will award to me on that day—and not only to me, but also to all who have longed for His appearing" (II Timothy 4:7-8).*

"Pray for us dearly, because we don't know about tomorrow," Pastor Lamb said. "We don't know when tribulation will come. Pray that our people might have strength to face persecution. They are threatened by the government with no salary or job if they attend the meetings, yet they still come. But please do not pray for the persecution to stop."

His last statement took me by surprise, but then I realized he saw persecution as a blessing. Every time they arrested him and sent him to prison, the church grew.

I asked Pastor Lamb how I could help him. He asked me to bring them more Bibles.

Over the years, I have visited him many times, each time bringing him a load of Bibles—sometimes sending them ahead in vans, and sometimes not even telling him their source.

But still, every time I have visited that special house church, I have looked around and seen only a few Bibles—the need is so great. People crowded around and peered over the shoulders of those who held the Bibles, just to follow along as the Word of God was read aloud.

On many occasions, I saw people holding torn pieces of paper. I soon realized these were pages from a Bible and shared in the group. This was not done out of disrespect for God's Word, but for the unquenchable desire to have a small portion of their very own.

On one of my visits, Pastor Lamb said the Public Security Bureau—the secret police—questioned him about my visit. They asked, "Why are you meeting with foreigners?"

"I am not," he said. "He is my brother."

One of the highlights of my life was one Sunday when Pastor Lamb invited me to speak to the Da Ma Zhan house church. He was my interpreter.

I am blessed to call Pastor Lamb my friend. He has endured more persecution than anyone I know. He was beaten and tortured for his faith—and yet he never wavered. Every time I am with him, he has a smile on his face and a song in his heart. He is God's gift to the underground church in China.

Samuel Lamb may be small in stature, but he is a giant of the faith to me.

CHAPTER FOURTEEN

bond . . . james bond

"EXPECT GREAT THINGS FROM GOD, ATTEMPT GREAT THINGS FOR GOD."

—WILLIAM CAREY[14]

In a communist country, you don't check anything in as a group. Airport personnel look at every piece of luggage, open every handbag, and check every passport. This was especially true going into China in the late 1980s.

I've been to China more than 20 times, but one always remembers the first time entering a new country. I was at Liberty University at the time. I was taking a group of students to the public schools in Hong Kong for evangelism and to sing in churches. Before leaving, I received a call from a staff member at Campus Crusade. He had heard about our trip to Hong Kong and our plans to travel into Mainland China for a few days of sightseeing. He asked if our students would be willing to take some Bibles from Hong Kong into Beijing. I told him we would be glad to. He asked the name of the hotel where we'd be staying and how many team members there would be.

My schedule took me to another country prior to the trip, and I arrived in Hong Kong a day after the students. As soon as I walked into the hotel, one of the Liberty staff members met me and said, "We've got a problem. Campus Crusade delivered the Bibles for Beijing. We've put them in your room, but you've got to come and see."

No big deal, or so I thought until I opened the door. The entire hotel room, from floor to ceiling, was crammed with Bibles. There was one small path leading from the door to the bed and to the bathroom. The room contained 10,000 Chinese Bibles. Everyone stood in the doorway, stunned. One student said, "What are we going to do with all these Bibles?"

As instinct kicked in, I sent some students out to buy a large duffle bag. When they returned, we were able to cram 90 Bibles into the bag, and so I figured, 10,000 Bibles divided by 90—that's 112 duffle bags we had to buy.

"How are we going to do this?" someone asked.

"I don't know," I said, "but we'll figure out a way."

Jonathan Falwell, one of the students and my roommate on this trip, said, "I've got my dad's credit card." I told him to hang on to it; we might need it.

Before we departed for the Hong Kong Airport, I told everyone to pack light, because we would all have to carry several duffle bags each. My only direction to them was, "Don't act like they're heavy." We arrived at the counter to check in, and attendants put the bags on the scales. "Sir, you are overweight," one said. "What have you got in these bags?"

I immediately responded, "Books! We're college students, and you know how college students love to read." I was praying the whole time that they wouldn't open the bags. The attendant told us it would be $1,150 in overweight charges. I turned around and said, "Okay, Jonathan, now I need your dad's credit card." I later told his dad, Jerry Falwell, "Thanks for the Bibles."

We arrived in Beijing. Picture this: 50 of us with 10,000 Bibles coming off the conveyor belt in bags—not too conspicuous. I kept thinking, "What am I doing? What have I gotten these students into?" I moved to a corner and prayed something like this: "God, if you've got a plan to get 10,000 Bibles past Chinese customs, now would be a good time to share it with me, because I don't have a clue."

While I was praying, I saw a huge luggage cart, the kind porters use. "Okay, you guys," I said, "let's get all the bags of 'bread' (we didn't want to use the word Bibles) and stack them on that luggage cart." We piled on the bags of bread, took off our jackets and laid them over the bags, and added some guitars on top. Two guys got on each end of the cart and we pushed it towards the counter. I told everyone, "Give me your passports, and I'll try to check us through customs as a group."

I walked up to the counter with dozens of American passports in my hand, a huge cart behind me, and a long trail of Liberty students. I smiled proudly and said, "Hi. We're college students from America. This is our first time in Beijing." I don't know whether I caught them off guard and messed up their routine, but they stuttered around, finally saying, "Okay. Welcome to China." We walked right in. I didn't hand them the passports, and they didn't even try to take the passports to stamp them. My friend Sumner Wemp was with me, and when we got out into the lobby and saw that the bread was behind us, he whispered in my ear, "Well . . . glory!"

A Chinese man walked up to me. I don't know how he knew me; I had never seen him before. He whispered in my other ear, "Place four bags on the sidewalk and go to your bus. We will contact you later at your hotel."

Man, I was pumped—I thought I was in a James Bond movie. I was made for this. We put four of the bags on the sidewalk and as we got on the bus, I was like Lot's wife—I had to turn around. I saw four Chinese men loading those four bags into four taxis and heading in four different directions.

When we got back to our room that night, I realized I didn't have any luggage. I had told everyone to pack light for our trip to Beijing so we could carry in those Bibles, but in my excitement I forgot to pack anything myself. No toothbrush, toothpaste, deodorant, change of clothes—nothing!

I sat on the edge of the bed, looking at the remaining bags of Bibles. "Jonathan," I said, "I wonder how God plans to distribute the rest of these Bibles?" We had only delivered a few of them, and we had very little time left.

About that time, there was a knock on the door. When I opened it, another Chinese man stood outside. He handed me a manila envelope. "Follow these instructions explicitly," he said, and left.

My juices started flowing again. Jonathan threw stuff off the bed and we spread out the envelope's contents. A cover letter said, "Half of your group will not feel like going to dinner tomorrow." (That wasn't a big deal; the students didn't like authentic Chinese food anyway.) "They will be conveniently absent. The half that doesn't go to dinner will break up into groups of two," the letter continued, "and make sure they follow their instructions explicitly."

One set of instructions said, "A group of four will each carry one bag out the front door of the hotel at precisely 8 p.m., get into a taxi that's waiting, and go wherever it takes you."

Now, that's my definition of faith.

The student body president of Liberty was in that group that night, and when they got back, I asked where he had gone. "Vernon," he said, "tonight was the most incredible night of my entire Christian life. We drove around town for an hour and pulled up to this little house church, and there was this 86-year-old woman leading a church service. She had been led to Christ by Watchman Nee." (Watchman Nee was one of the early Chinese Christians who started the whole revival movement in China, and the writer of probably one of the greatest Christian books ever written, *The Normal Christian Life*.)

He continued, "When we got there, they were all on their knees praying for Bibles. When we walked in with these four bags, they hugged and kissed us and made us sit down, and we had a three-hour house church service. It was indescribable."

The instructions for my group said, "Go out the side door at precisely 8 p.m. and walk four blocks." I should have read it more carefully. We were carrying two bags each. Wes Tuttle, his wife Bernee, and I carried 200 pounds of Bibles for four blocks. I told Wes that I could just see the headlines the next day: "Vice president of Liberty University survives cancer and dies of heart attack on the streets of Beijing."

As we stood on the street corner, Wes asked, "What do we do now?" I got out my piece of paper. It just said, "Wait," so we waited for 30 minutes. Finally, a van pulled up and the side door slid open.

A Chinese man said, "Get in." We drove around town for about an hour to make sure we weren't followed. We ended up at a university. We went to the back of the university to a dorm, and carried those Bibles up three flights of stairs. We knocked on the door, and a Chinese student let us in. He took us to his room where we unpacked the Bibles. You could tell he was excited as he carefully touched each one.

The student spoke to us in English. "By this time tomorrow," he said, "these Bibles will be distributed throughout this campus." We held hands and prayed over them.

Ultimately, all the Bibles were successfully delivered without incident.

That was May, 1989. I got home jet lagged, tired, and fulfilled. On June 5, I turned on CNN and saw thousands of Beijing college students assembled at Tiananmen Square, standing up to their government. I'll never forget that one student who stood in front of a tank, defying the Chinese army. I had to believe that of the 4,000 students murdered that night in Tiananmen Square, some of them had to be believers who received the Bibles we delivered just a few weeks before.

CHAPTER FIFTEEN

one million bibles for china

"I AM NOT ASHAMED OF THE GOSPEL, BECAUSE IT IS
THE POWER OF GOD FOR THE SALVATION OF EVERYONE
WHO BELIEVES."

—ROMANS 1:16

"Try not to attract too much attention to yourself," my Chinese friends told me as we walked out the front door of the hotel, "and don't talk too much." This was not an easy task for me, but I did my best to act naturally.

I was back in Beijing, which was bustling with activity at the onset of rush hour traffic. We walked for several blocks without talking then darted into another hotel. After about five minutes, we scurried out the door again and into a taxi. Thirty minutes later, we got out again.

We crossed the street and got into yet another taxi and traveled around the city with no particular destination. After a while, we got out and just stood on the busy street corner for another 15 minutes until a small mini-van pulled up. We all piled in.

Our Chinese friends covered us with blankets and told us to lie down and keep out of sight. "Please don't say a word or make a sound," they said. We drove to the outskirts of Beijing and up to the front gate of a Chinese retirement home and quickly pulled the van into the courtyard.

It seemed like "Cloak and Dagger," but our friends insisted we could not be followed or detected. We were about to find out why.

We quickly ran into the building and were greeted by more than 40 underground Chinese pastors and Christian leaders. Excited to see us, they welcomed us warmly with hugs and huge smiles. We then discovered we would not be allowed to leave the compound for two days.

Millions of Christians in China have refused to register with the government because of all the restrictions. In many places, authorities tell registered pastors what they can and cannot say in their sermons. In other places, they're not allowed to evangelize anyone under the age of 18. Religious freedom is for the "government sanctioned" churches only—those churches that say and do only what the government allows.

One Chinese pastor told me, "Jesus is not the head of the registered churches, the government is."

Christians who refuse to register face extreme persecution and are forced to meet secretly underground. In a real sense, they are "God's Underground Church."

Almost all the leaders we met were severely beaten for their faith and spent time in prison, some for as long as five years. We were humbled to be in their presence.

One group of Chinese brothers and sisters traveled 28 hours one way to meet with us.

We were escorted into a small room and introduced to the leader of one of the largest house church movements in China. He was also one of the most wanted men in China.

He told us that although it's true that many Chinese own a Bible, he estimated that as many as 80 million Chinese Christians still did not have a copy of God's Word—unbelievable.

This persecuted pastor asked me for one million Bibles.

Prompted by the Holy Spirit, I said, "Yes."

We shook hands and prayed, then he left, not wanting to risk capture in the presence of foreigners.

For the next two days, we sat in a locked room, never leaving the building for security reasons. We couldn't use our real names, and our Chinese friends didn't tell us their real names or where they lived. If we faced interrogation by the police, there would be no way for us to endanger them. They gave me the name, "Peter."

One Chinese pastor, "Paul," told me he was the pastor of 20 different house churches in seven separate villages. He was arrested and spent the first four months of his incarceration in handcuffs. He was interrogated every day and beaten, yet he still refused to renounce his faith. Paul spent three years in prison and was forced to perform difficult physical labor, but he still had a smile on his face.

Another leader, "Timothy," told me how difficult it was to find Bibles, so he copied the entire Bible by hand. Caught later by the police, he spent more than five years in prison—his only crime was making a copy of the Bible.

Two of the pastors we met were arrested the day after we left—caught in a Beijing train station while trying to return home.

When I arrived at our hotel after two exhausting days of teaching, praying, and worshipping God, a Chinese worker slipped a piece of paper into my hand. I didn't open it until I reached my room. As I read the handwritten note from our Chinese partner, "Barnabas," the regular, ongoing persecution these godly men and women face came into sharp focus.

Dear Peter and other brothers,

Please pray for two pastors who were arrested this morning. Most others who attended the meeting escaped. Some may have problems or are also being arrested, but we don't know yet.

Please pray hard for the two pastors and others who are arrested, that they will be released soon. Others are running. Pray for their safety.

Take care, brothers. This is risky business here in China, but it is worth it to do, even though I might have to give up my life. But God is in control.

Pray . . . pray . . . pray!

Your brother in Christ,
Barnabas

The next day, we worshipped in a house church of over 2,000 members where more than 90 Chinese crammed into one small room. The 87-year-old pastor sat on the side of his bed in the corner and used the kitchen table as his pulpit. I listened to them pray and worship God in song. The leaders asked me to speak—it was an amazing experience. Twenty of the members also hold house church meetings in their homes.

One woman gave me her personal *handwritten* Bible and commentary. I didn't want to take it, because I knew the sacrifice she had made to write each verse by hand. But she insisted that I keep it to remember her by. "Let it become a reminder of the urgency to get more Bibles into China," she said.

I didn't know then how we would ever get the resources to print one million Bibles. I didn't know how many of our friends would be moved to help us—but God knew.

When I returned home, I told our friends these amazing

stories and how desperately these believers needed Bibles. But I couldn't tell anyone the details of how we would print and distribute them, because to do so would place our Chinese brothers and sisters in further jeopardy. All I could tell them was that these Bibles would be printed inside China by several different printers in small quantities throughout the country to avoid raising suspicion.

One of my Chinese brothers, "John," told me that each Bible provided would touch the lives of 300 people, and on average, 10 Chinese would come to Christ. When Chinese Christians finally receive their own Bibles, they are excited and go door to door, reading Scriptures to all of their family and friends. This is how many of the house churches are started.

Every time I visit China, I learn something new. I'm often amazed that well-meaning American Christians say there is religious freedom in China—that persecution no longer exists.

And although there may be many places where this is true, it is not an accurate picture of the entire country. I remember the story of four blind men who each touched an elephant and then tried to describe it. One touched the trunk, one touched the tail, one touched a leg, and the last touched the stomach. Each blind man had a different perspective.

I have heard firsthand about the persecution and suffering from my brothers and sisters in China. I know that persecution still exists there.

I received this report on persecution in China:

> We have heard a rumor that, overseas, people are saying that there is no longer any persecution in China. We find this hard to believe. There are more than 100 pastors in

prison here, and many young Christians under eighteen that are under strong pressure from the police. Some were thrown into manure pits, others were beaten with electric stun-batons, and some were beaten so they could not stand.

Persecution is normal for us.

Overseas, Christians say the gospel is flourishing in China because people have lost faith in Marxism and because of material poverty. These are certainly reasons. But I believe deeply that we have paid a great price for the gospel—much blood and sweat and many tears.

The Word of God is held in great esteem and highly cherished among house church Christians. Bibles are still very scarce in some areas and there is a great hunger among the people of God for the Scriptures.

It is not merely for the pleasure of being able to read the Bible that we long to own a copy. We are desperate to understand God's heart on many issues. We want to be doers of the Word, not merely hearers.

Bibles are like gold dust, virtually unobtainable for many Christians. That is why portions of Scripture are still copied out by hand, many times over, and distributed to as many people as possible. These portions will sometimes be memorized thoroughly. You discover just how much has been remembered when we pray—for the Word of God is liberally

mixed into our prayers.
Chinese Christians love God's Word.

One of World Help's core values is "Accomplishing God-Sized Tasks That Last for Eternity." It took us more than two years to accomplish the God-sized task of providing one million Bibles for China. We reached our goal and now millions of Chinese have access to God's Word.

CHAPTER SIXTEEN

with all due respect

"DON'T BE UPSET WHEN THEY HAUL YOU BEFORE THE CIVIL AUTHORITIES. WITHOUT KNOWING IT, THEY'VE DONE YOU—AND ME—A FAVOR, GIVEN YOU A PLATFORM FOR PREACHING THE KINGDOM NEWS! AND DON'T WORRY ABOUT WHAT YOU'LL SAY OR HOW YOU'LL SAY IT. THE RIGHT WORDS WILL BE THERE; THE SPIRIT OF YOUR FATHER WILL SUPPLY THE WORDS."

—MATTHEW 10:18-20, THE MESSAGE

The secret police said, "Come with me," and led us to a small room filled with 12 government officials. For nearly two hours, we were interrogated harshly.

Jay Strack had joined me in Havana, Cuba, on a humanitarian aid mission. We took more than 300 pounds of medical supplies to Havana, but as soon as government officials realized our cargo was earmarked for churches, they called us in for questioning.

They detained us for three hours. It would have been slightly shorter, but after two hours of lecturing and indoctrination about the superiority of communism over capitalism, I couldn't keep quiet.

"Cuba enjoys religious freedom," our interrogators said.

I wish now I had just kept my mouth shut, but I immediately blurted out, "With all due respect, Cuba does not have religious freedom."

Jay rolled his eyes as if to say, "Vernon, why couldn't you just be quiet?"

Another lengthy tirade of communistic propaganda followed, "Cuba is a free nation. We have no problems here."

But what we saw with our own eyes proved them wrong.

We were told, "You cannot preach in Cuba. You cannot pray in a public church service. You cannot distribute Bibles or you will be deported."

They were serious. In fact, our Canadian friend who met us at the airport was detained for nearly 24 hours, arrested, and deported the next day—he wasn't even allowed to contact his embassy.

In our travels there, we saw constant reminders of what Russia was like before the Berlin Wall came down. Cuba's economy faced bankruptcy, the government was corrupt, and Fidel Castro clung tightly to his power.

Cuba is still essentially a communist country, one of the last holdouts of the "Cold War." Before Castro's revolution, Cubans enjoyed one of the highest standards of living in all of Latin America, but now people wait for hours in long lines for public transportation and often go hungry. We saw the crumbling infrastructure, poverty, filth, and despair.

It was a sad indictment to godless communism.

We walked through the streets of Havana, wondering how to deal with the secret police who followed us closely, monitoring our every move. We saw very young girls (probably not even in their teens) in beautiful dresses walking the streets. We realized they were prostitutes for the foreign tourists.

In the days that followed, we met with pastors and Christian leaders who told us about Cuba's unusual revival. They shared that every day more than 1,000 Cubans were becoming Christ followers, in spite of rigid communist control. New house churches were starting every day and many churches had doubled their attendance within a year.

I also met several pastors who spent as many as five years in prison. They certainly had my attention and respect.

Although the pastors and Christian leaders explained that their greatest need was more Bibles, we knew it was illegal to print Bibles in Cuba, and it was illegal for foreigners to openly distribute them. But we learned that Cuban Christians could distribute Bibles freely. The only problem was—there were no Bibles to distribute.

On the plane ride home, I realized God took me to Cuba to open my eyes. I asked Him to allow me to help provide the Bibles those Cuban pastors and new believers needed.

It wasn't long until I received an answer from God.

In May and June of 1999, for the first time in more than three decades, Fidel Castro gave permission for Protestant churches to conduct 18 open-air evangelistic celebrations. He also agreed to allow the distribution of Bibles and Christian literature during the celebrations.

Everything happened so fast. We only had a short time to raise funds to provide Bibles for these unprecedented events, but God answered our prayers. World Help provided more than 50,000 Spanish Bibles for these celebrations.

My second trip to Cuba was quite a contrast from the first. There were no interrogations, secret police, or three-hour lectures. I walked right through customs without a hitch.

Everywhere I went in Havana, I saw announcements of the events on massive billboards. This was the first time their billboards announced a Christian celebration.

Over 500,000 Cubans attended these historic events, and four of the celebrations were broadcast live on nationwide television and radio. Millions of Cubans heard the Good News for the first time.

I met one of the pastors who gave the first evangelistic message on Cuban television. He had spent two years in a labor camp after being married for only five months.

"[The labor camp] was my schooling to prepare me for the work God had for Cuba," he said. "We had to go through many difficult times in order for God to use us."

Two nights before the final celebration in Havana, Castro met with the pastors' organization committee. He wanted to know how the meetings were going and seemed genuinely interested. The pastors asked him to attend the final celebration.

I arrived at the plaza two hours early that morning. There were already thousands of people gathered by the time I got there. Christians came in groups of hundreds. They sang, carried signs, distributed tracts, and chanted, *"Cristo Vive! Cristo Vive!"*—"Christ Lives!"

I asked myself, "Is this really happening?" It felt like a dream.

A large sign with the words "Jesus Christ for All and by All" stood a few hundred yards from a towering image of the late revolutionary Che Guevara, one of Cuba's most famous atheists.

If I hadn't seen it with my own eyes, I wouldn't have believed it. Wearing his traditional olive green fatigues and cap, Fidel Castro sat on the front row in Havana's Revolution Square with members of his Cabinet.

He stayed for the entire celebration while the Gospel was presented clearly in song, testimony, Scripture, and sermon. Castro seemed genuinely moved as an 8-year-old girl quoted the entire chapter of Isaiah 55 in Spanish and as over 150,000 Cubans stood to their feet and sang, "How Great Thou Art."

At the close of the celebration, one elderly pastor told me, "This is just the beginning of God's blessing after 40 years of hardship. We are prepared for the great spiritual harvest God is bringing to our nation."

CHAPTER SEVENTEEN

good morning, vietnam

"WHEN CHRIST CALLS A MAN, HE BIDS HIM COME AND DIE."

—DIETRICH BONHOEFFER[15]

As my plane landed in Ho Chi Minh City (many still call it Saigon), I didn't know what to expect. I saw visible reminders of a war from three decades earlier. Most Vietnamese weren't even born in 1965 when the U.S. sent in the first troops; all they know is communism.

No photos were allowed at the airport, but the sight was unforgettable. It was hot and humid; there were crowds of people and palm trees in the distance. I felt that if I closed my eyes I would hear the roar of helicopter blades and see young American soldiers preparing to die. It was too surreal. I expected to hear Robin Williams yell out at any moment, "Good Morning, Vietnam!"

Within a few hours of arriving, our guide took the entire team to a secret location. We met with some courageous men and women—introduced to us only as our "friends." We could not call them pastors, mention God, bow our heads to pray, or even open our Bibles.

Our guide requested that we not ask them their real names or the area where they worked; and we were not allowed to take any photographs of our friends. To do so would put them in danger.

The first person we met was "Elizabeth," a young woman evangelist and church planter. Arrested six times by the secret police, she suffered many brutal beatings. She was detained for weeks at a time, paraded through the streets for people to mock and fined six month's salary.

At one time her persecutors tied her hands and threw her from a boat in the river . . . she almost drowned. They forced her to march up and down a mountain for days. The police repeatedly threatened to kill her. They beat her on the head saying, "You are so stupid to believe in Jesus Christ. Even a dog is smarter than you." Her strength to endure came from God.

I didn't have a clue how to respond—all I could do was sit there in shock at what I was hearing.

Then Pastor "Joseph" broke the silence, sharing his own story. Three years earlier he traveled to a remote tribal area where there were only four Christians.

"Today, I pastor six churches with 287 believers," he said. "The government will not give me land for a house to meet in or allow the Christians' children to attend school. I was arrested six months ago for refusing to forsake Christ."

The pastor was released just a few days before we arrived. I felt so unworthy to be in the presence of these persecuted friends.

I was amazed to hear that many of the children who accept Christ are beaten by their parents. But after the parents see the change in their children, many of them also come to Christ.

Pastor "Mark" from the Mekong Delta region explained that a Lieutenant Colonel in the Vietnamese army came into his church to tear it down. The soldier grabbed a chair to throw it out, but started shaking uncontrollably. Fearful, he ran out. The next day he came back and said, "You are worshipping the true God. I will leave you alone."

It was obvious—these men and women experienced the

power of God on a regular basis.

I discovered that one of the foremost Christian leaders in the country—responsible for overseeing more than 1,000 churches— was in the room. He told us the story of a pastor working in a remote tribal area.

Police came with pre-printed forms stating, "I will forsake Christianity and re-establish my ancestral family altar." They threatened to kill all 430 Christians in that village if they refused to sign the statement. Because they were afraid, they reluctantly signed the document but immediately fled the area. All 40 families packed up their few belongings and traveled more than 1,000 miles to a remote region in the mountains where they re-established their homes.

Now the mountain families have started several house churches. When one of their Christian friends found out where they had moved, he asked them, "How do you feel?"

They said, "Now we have freedom to worship."

As I heard the stories of these dedicated believers, I imagined what it must have been like for Christians in the first century church. This wonderful Christian leader sitting next to me spent seven years in prison because another pastor, an informant, turned him in. I couldn't even imagine what it must feel like to live in an atmosphere of fear and distrust.

The next day, nine more friends met with us. "Peter," 35 years old and a pastor—but a Christian for only one year—had already experienced great persecution. He and his wife were beaten many times. The authorities burned down their house because he wouldn't forsake Christ. He built a tent and the authorities burned that down too.

Peter moved into another tent with his wife and four children. With tears in his eyes, he said, "My pregnant wife was once again severely beaten. She lost our baby."

We were all so humbled. No one said a word.

A 34-year-old woman evangelist and church planter related her story of continued persecution. One day the police publicly humiliated her by tearing off her shirt and parading her through the streets. She stood in that public gathering, half naked with her hands tied behind her back and said, "I live for Jesus Christ . . . if I die, I die for Jesus Christ!"

After a short, sleepless night, we got up early and traveled five hours to another remote area where the Communists destroyed three church buildings.

We arrived at a tribal village of thatched houses where we secretly met with 10 Christ followers. For security reasons, we could only stay 15 minutes. We didn't want an informant to see us and report these Christians to the authorities. It seems illogical—we drove five hours to meet with them for only 15 minutes. But their smiles and handshakes told us we had encouraged them just by being there.

We knelt and prayed with these faithful servants, realizing they would probably be arrested and beaten because of our presence.

It was only three days, but I had the extraordinary opportunity to talk with 52 of the most committed pastors, evangelists, and church planters I'll probably ever meet. They call themselves "God's Silent Church." How could I ever forget them?

On the drive home, we traveled down the "Bloody Highway" where the worst battles of the Vietnam War were fought.

I bowed my head and prayed:

> *God, you have my attention. Help me to see and feel their suffering so very real in my own life that I cannot forget what I have seen and felt. I can't even begin to imagine what these*

dear Christians suffer daily; they are sacrificing so much for you. My faith and commitment pales by comparison. Never let me become complacent and comfortable again. Thank you for refocusing my attention on what is really important in this life and what really matters.

Amen.

CHAPTER EIGHTEEN

god i can't . . . it's too big

"IF YOU TELL SOMEONE YOUR VISION AND THEY DON'T LAUGH, IT'S NOT BIG ENOUGH."

—JOHN MAXWELL

It was March of 1996 and my first day in India—what an eye-opening experience. By that time, I had already traveled around the world for many years, so I thought I had seen it all. I was no stranger to poverty, filth, and spiritual darkness, but nothing in my travels prepared me for what I experienced in India.

After traveling 38 hours, we arrived in New Delhi, a city of over 11 million people. I was overwhelmed by the masses of people everywhere I looked. The poverty, the stench, and the hopelessness on their faces were an all-out assault on my senses.

People were starving as "sacred" cows walked down the streets. Children roamed about with little, if any, clothing. People slept in cardboard boxes, and filthy sewage filled the streets. I saw the worst traffic and driving conditions imaginable, pollution, trash everywhere, and an unmistakable sense of spiritual oppression. I was in culture shock.

I wasn't sure why God sent me to India, but He sure had my attention.

We took a seven-hour train ride from Delhi to a remote part of Rajasthan, home to the maharajas. At the train station, there were thousands of people—diseased, blind, crippled, poor, and destitute—it was overwhelming. Before I left the U.S., I asked God to break my heart with the things that break His heart—and He certainly did.

I took a few minutes to catch my breath, then we were off again for a bumpy six-hour ride in an old jeep. When we finally reached our destination, I was exhausted and totally out of my comfort zone but excited about what God was going to do.

The next morning in India, our small team drove about an hour out of town to the remote village of Karpina. I was told there wasn't a church within 50 miles in any direction. I met a young pastor who discipled 192 new believers in only 14 months. They were meeting together under a tree; they didn't have a church building.

That's why we were there.

We dedicated an unfinished building provided by a group of Liberty University students. It was only 9 a.m., yet more than 200 people arrived to witness this unusual event. Some walked as far as 20 miles one way to attend. The pastor had no car—not even a bicycle—yet he had already accomplished so much.

Another young pastor told me, "We have a thousand pastors trained and ready right now to plant a thousand new churches. All we need is some help."

It was then I heard the still small voice of God saying, "Vernon, this is why I brought you to India. This is why I spared your life from cancer and gave you a new lease on life. This is why World Help was started. This is what I want you to do for the rest of your life—plant churches where no churches exist."

I quickly did the math in my mind . . . $4,000 to build one church building multiplied by 1,000 trained pastors . . . that's $4 MILLION DOLLARS!

I prayed silently, "God, I can't do this. It's too big!" And once again I heard that small voice of God say, "Good . . . I can!"

I soon discovered there were over 600,000 villages in India, and the vast majority didn't have a church of any kind. God's vision for me was clear—1,000 new churches. To make sure I would follow through, I set a deadline to complete the vision by the year 2000. That very day, *Vision 1000* was born.

I returned home so excited. When I told my family and friends what I had experienced and my vision to see 1,000 new churches planted and 1,000 new buildings built by the year 2000, some of them laughed.

John Maxwell once told me, "Vernon, if you tell someone your vision and they don't laugh, it's not big enough."

One of my board members tried to bring me back to my senses by suggesting I lower the goal to 200 churches, but it didn't work. My vision from God was clear—crystal clear!

My wife Patty and I knew if I was going to spend the next few years asking people to help make this vision a reality, we needed to provide the first church ourselves. I had just purchased a really nice, used car, but we decided to sell it. We drove an older car for over a year—but it sure was worth it.

The funds we sent to India were used to build a church building in a city of at least 200,000 people. It was the only church in the entire city. We decided to dedicate it in honor of my parents Fred and Vivian Brewer for their more than 50 years of dedicated service to the ministry.

They were incredibly happy. I even helped them raise the funds to go to India for the dedication—it was quite the event. More than 1,000 people showed up. Even local and state government officials were there. They had never experienced a church building dedication, so they thought they were just supposed to be there.

At the last minute, I was asked to speak. I shared a simple message about God's love and explained that Jesus Christ died and rose from the dead. Many Hindu men and women became Christ followers that night.

I will never forget the look of joy on my parents' faces as they saw the vision God had so clearly given me begin to become a reality.

A few months later, I was back in India. The pastor of the church we helped build identified 20 villages surrounding their city, established house churches in each village, and already had more than 300 baptized believers.

One by one, God brought people across my path to make the vision possible. I soon learned that when the vision is God's—He will make it happen. Churches caught the vision. Friends, family members, and people I didn't even know wanted to be part of something bigger than themselves.

A year later, my wife's father died. He was one of the finest Christian men I knew. One day, not long after the funeral, while I prepared to leave for a trip, Patty sat on the steps and began to cry. I thought she was sad because I was leaving. But instead she said, "I miss my Dad. Could we build another church in India," she asked, "this time in memory of him?"

We looked out the door to the driveway where my beautiful black Jeep Wrangler was parked. It had a soft top, four-wheel drive, chrome wheels, a CD player—it was loaded and I looked pretty good driving in it. (Can you tell I was emotionally attached?)

We soon decided to sell that one too, and we sent the money to India. This time our gift went to the city of Alwar, and a new church building was built where no church existed. But at the time we didn't realize the significance of Alwar.

Alwar is not the best place to start a new church. In fact, the name Alwar actually means "the city which housed the throne of Satan." It was a strong anti-Christian city.

Many years ago, an evangelist named Dori Raj went to Alwar to start a church. The militant Hindus said, "If you don't leave, we will kill you." Dori Raj replied, "God has called me here, and I will not leave."

They did kill Dori Raj and his body was never found. At his memorial service, his 8-year-old nephew Solomon stood up to address the crowd.

"Someday I will go work for Christ in Alwar where my uncle died," he said, "and I will die also, if necessary." When Solomon grew up, he went away to Bible College. After he graduated, he did as he promised and went to Alwar to start a church. He used the money we sent to build a church building.

My family was privileged to be in Alwar to dedicate that new church building. Somehow, I knew that looking down from heaven were at least two very happy men—Dori Raj, the martyred pastor; and Glen Bentley, my wife's father, a coal miner from West Virginia.

For several years, I cast this vision everywhere I went and people caught it.

On December 31, 1999, we were still 10 churches away from reaching our goal. I was home when the phone rang. Someone I didn't even know called to tell me he was mailing a check for $40,000 to build 10 new churches. I looked at my watch. It was 1:27 in the afternoon. We did it with plenty of time to spare.

I have always said, "God is seldom early, but never late." This time, He was early.

But, as I watched CNN bring in the new millennium around the world, I realized that with the unusual 10-and-a-half hour time difference in India, it was actually midnight in New Delhi. And then it hit me. God did it—He did it on India time.

photojournal

That's me on the left in 1965 distributing New Testaments
in Mexico . . . the first of many defining moments.

My daughters Noel and Nikki with Nildo on the streets of Rio de Janeiro

With Jerry Falwell at Moscow's Red Square

Presenting a mini-library to a Russian pastor

At the Berlin Wall

Nikki and my son Josh inside the Kremlin

World Help board member Skip Taylor delivering food to a forgotten village in Thailand

Presenting the Gospel on a Russian military base

The Ganges River in Varanasi, India

Skip Taylor and I with the boys of Maru Asha

Josh with the Vice President of Uganda

With Jonathan Falwell on the streets of Hong Kong

World Help team at the pyramids

Pastor Kam with the believers in Chaku, Nepal

Fidel Castro listening to the Gospel in Revolution Square

With Tom Thompson at the Great Wall of China

Sharing the Gospel with 50,000 in Ghujarat, India

Distributing Bibles to the Russian military

My wife Patty in a Ugandan village

Nikki and her husband Mark with James and Moite at Gilgal Children's Home

My daughter Jenny with children from a Kenyan village

World Help team praying over Samuel Lamb in Guangzhou

The day I climbed Mt. Everest . . . well . . .

Historic gathering of nearly 400 Russian pastors and
16 American pastors ministering side by side

Noel with children from the Child Sponsorship Program in Rwanda

Meeting with house church members in Beijing

Children from World Help's Child Sponsorship Program in the Philippines

With my dad Fred Brewer at a children's home in India

Josh with the Forgotten Children of Northern Uganda

With Iraqi soldiers near Mosul

Distributing gifts in Northern Iraq

Giving hope to children in Zambia

Patty and I on the Ganges River

With Tom in a Nepali village

All three *Children of the World* teams with Jonathan Falwell
at Thomas Road Baptist Church

The late Allen Yuan, a leader of China's House Church Movement

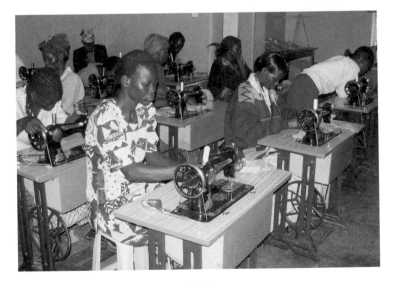

Vocational training for Uganda's Forgotten Children

Joni and friends in front of St. Basil's Cathedral in Moscow's Red Square

CHAPTER NINETEEN

rollin' down the river

"LORD, MAKE ME AN INSTRUMENT OF YOUR PEACE;
WHERE THERE IS HATRED, LET ME SOW LOVE;
WHERE THERE IS INJURY, PARDON;
WHERE THERE IS DOUBT, FAITH;
WHERE THERE IS DESPAIR, HOPE;
WHERE THERE IS DARKNESS, LIGHT;
AND WHERE THERE IS SADNESS, JOY."

—ST. FRANCIS OF ASSISI[16]

My alarm went off at 4:30 a.m.—way too early for my jet-lagged, exhausted body. But this was one morning I just couldn't sleep in. I was in India and I wanted to be on the Ganges River by dawn.

As I walked through the dark streets near the river, I stumbled over people who had spent the night sleeping on the streets. Beggars were already waiting with their hands out for food, money, or anything else they could get. The sight of filthy and starving children begging for food was hard to bear.

By the time I arrived at the riverbank, thousands of people were already washing themselves in the filthy water. Hindus believe if they ceremoniously bathe in this most holy of all rivers, their sins will be washed away.

But the waters of the Ganges are polluted by raw sewage,

trash, animal carcasses, dead bodies, and the ashes of cremated humans. Every day more than 100 bodies are burned in Varanasi and their ashes are sprinkled in the river. Hindus believe this allows their loved ones direct access to heaven. I saw piles of wood, the smoke from the burning bodies, and family members weeping with little or no hope.

I boarded a small boat with our team and we slowly floated up and down the river. No one spoke a word. I think we were shocked and sickened at what we witnessed.

I saw people up to their waist in the river, pouring water on their heads; and some were actually drinking it. They were drinking disease! Some used brass pots to scoop up water, hold them above their heads and slowly pour it over themselves. They were so sincere. Many folded their hands and prayed. Hindu holy men with painted faces and bright orange clothing chanted, while music played in the background. All of these activities were sincere acts of worship as they asked for forgiveness.

I was overwhelmed! The masses of humanity—diseased, blind, crippled, poor, and destitute—were all around me. Children, the neediest of the needy, were orphaned and neglected. They filled the streets, having no one to care for them and no place to call home.

Just a few miles away in the city of Allahabad, the holiest city in Hinduism, 60 million devout Hindus gathered for the annual Kumbh Mela—a celebration and pilgrimage for faithful Hindus. These Hindu pilgrims came to the banks of the Ganges River in the false hope that if they were sincere enough their sins would be forgiven.

However, God is breaking through this spiritual darkness. I witnessed more than 40,000 Indian seekers singing, praying, and responding to the Gospel. It was incredible to worship with thousands of former Hindus who are now Christ followers. Just a few years ago, there were only 500 known believers in all of Allahabad. But today, thousands come every week to worship Jesus Christ—the largest Christian gathering in all of India.

I prayed with their leadership that day, and they told me their plans to plant churches in every unreached city and village of Northern India. I knew, "This is where God is working," and He wanted me to join Him there.

I also met with about 70 of our World Help church planters in a secluded location. As I drove from village to village, I counted at least 40 Hindu shrines and temples within just a few miles, but I didn't see one single Christian church building—not even one. Hindus and Muslims taunt new Christ followers, saying, "If your God is so great, why don't you have a place to worship Him?"

We made plans to provide multipurpose church buildings for each village. On Sundays, they are used for worship, but the rest of the week they provide space for village schools and meeting places. The villagers take great pride in these buildings.

These church planters meet together once a month for three days of training, strategizing, and encouragement. World Help's Senior Vice President Tom Thompson shared words of encouragement as we prayed and worshipped with them. They told us amazing stories to illustrate how God is building His kingdom in Northern India, and how more than 5,600 new churches were planted there in only one year and thousands of new Christ followers were baptized.

One of our church planters, Zul Fakar, was working in a dangerous, persecuted area when militant anti-Christians ambushed him in an alley and beat him to death. He died on August 10. That's my birthday, so I will always be reminded of his sacrifice. He was a believer for only 15 months, but before his death he already had 25 converts and two churches established in unreached villages.

His wife, Rabia, was strongly encouraged to deny her faith and come back to her home village. She bravely refused. "My husband died for his faith in Jesus Christ," she said. "The best way I can honor his memory is to spend my life serving the One he died for."

It was a sobering reminder that these church planters are in life-and-death situations every day as they take the Good News to villages that have no churches.

I prayed as I floated down the filthy Ganges River early that morning, overwhelmed by the spiritual darkness that totally enveloped us. I prayed for our church planters. I asked God to continue to give them courage and boldness and to use them to shine the light of God into all of India's spiritual darkness. I prayed as I walked down the streets, looking into the faces of thousands of sincere idol worshippers. I realized that no one had ever told them that it isn't the dirty, polluted waters of the Ganges River that wash away their sins, but only the shed blood of Jesus Christ.

They have never heard of Jesus. They have never heard the Good News—not even one time. They are totally unreached. I asked God to open their eyes.

CHAPTER TWENTY

maru asha

"VISION IS SEEING THE INVISIBLE AND MAKING IT VISIBLE."

—VERNON BREWER

I magine yourself as an 11-year-old child with three younger siblings. You're abandoned in a railway station, surrounded by thousands of strangers. You're all alone with no one to help. Think about how hopeless and scared you would feel.

These were the heartbreaking circumstances that Trevor DeLinares faced at such a young, vulnerable age. Trevor's father had a good job as an engineer. His family appeared to have a good life, but his father was an alcoholic who beat Trevor's mother every day when he came home from work. The children grew up in constant fear of him.

When Trevor's mother abandoned her family, his father quit his job and began drinking even more. One day he told the children to pack their belongings; they were all going to live with a close relative. He took his four children to one of the most crowded and dangerous railway stations in all of India and left them there alone, promising to return with tickets—but he never came back. Like his wife, he also abandoned the children.

They stayed there for three days—stranded with no money, food, or water, and surrounded by a mass of people. They were terrified and alone. Finally, a policeman came to their rescue, and they eventually were taken to a Christian orphanage in Northern

India where they received the unconditional love, care, and education they desperately needed.

God gave Trevor a new life at that children's home. He also transformed Trevor's living nightmare into the dream of one day providing a loving home for other hurting boys and girls, just like him.

Trevor received an education and grew into a fine, young, committed Christian. His life, which seemed so hopeless, found a new beginning in Christ. Trevor knew God had a plan for his life, and he knew he had a passion to help hopeless, needy children. That desire never left him.

On my first day in India, I dedicated a church in an unreached village, and Trevor was my interpreter. As I got to know him, he shared his vision to care for the abandoned and forgotten children in India's slums. I heard the passion in his voice as he told me about the desperate needs of the children who go for days without food and water—thousands of hungry boys and girls who sleep on the rat-infested streets of India's mega-cities. I knew that someday God would use this young man for His glory. Since that day in the desert village, Trevor became not only a ministry partner, but also my faithful friend.

Trevor and I both knew he had no way to take on this incredible responsibility alone. He needed help.

Because Trevor was so sincere and the need was so compelling, I promised to help him. I told him I would provide a home for these children who have only known a life of abject poverty, disease, and fear. I didn't know how I was going to do it—all I knew was God wanted me to be a part of Trevor's vision.

Within a few months, we supplied a temporary rented facility with room for 15 children, providing them with shelter, education, and a loving home. Although it was a small beginning, Trevor knew he would make a difference, not just for these first 15 children, but hopefully for hundreds more.

His passion to help children has not diminished. In fact, it continues to grow. Trevor's ultimate vision is to see a Christian school and children's home in Kalwar, just outside of Jaipur, a city of 2.5 million. He envisions at least 500 children in this school and orphanage someday.

We prayed for the resources to buy the land, as well as to build girls' and boys' homes where these children can have a safe place to live. We also prayed for a kitchen and dining room where they can be fed, and a school where they can be taught Christian values.

Beyond homes and facilities to care for the children, we want to help Trevor plant a new church and construct a new church building in the same village where his children's home will be located. Just think—children, their parents, and other relatives will all be able to hear the Gospel and see it in action every day. Trevor's vision is to see an entire village transformed by the Gospel. God is answering our prayers.

I recently returned to India to dedicate the new property Trevor purchased as a result of the many generous gifts from World Help's friends, and now the building process for the homes, classrooms, and chapel has begun. Trevor's vision is quickly becoming a reality.

God made something beautiful out of Trevor's life, and the name of his new children's home says it all—"Maru Asha" means Desert Hope.

Vision is seeing the invisible and making it visible.

Let me tell you what I see. I see hundreds of boys and girls that have known only poverty and fear learning that God loves them and cares for them.

I see the land. I see the buildings where these boys and girls will be fed, sheltered, educated, and loved. I see tomorrow's teachers, doctors, and nurses. I see future church planters and pastors. Can you see them? I can.

And if I look really hard, I can see that scared little boy standing on the platform at the Bombay train station . . . not knowing that someday God would use him to change the world.

CHAPTER TWENTY-ONE

if you are still here tomorrow, we will kill you

"MY GOD IS MY ROCK, IN WHOM I TAKE REFUGE, MY
SHIELD AND THE HORN OF MY SALVATION. HE IS MY
STRONGHOLD, MY REFUGE AND MY SAVIOR—FROM
VIOLENT MEN YOU SAVE ME."

—II SAMUEL 22:3

My phone rang in the middle of the night. I wasn't quite awake yet when I heard the trembling voice on the other end. It was our partner Kam, calling from Nepal. He talked so fast I had a difficult time understanding him. He was obviously shaken and scared.

But then his words sunk in—his life had been threatened. Not only that, the 52 orphans he cares for were also threatened.

The Maoist terrorists barged into his home uninvited, carrying guns, and shouting, "We want you out of here now, and if you are still here tomorrow, we will kill you." It was a terrifying situation, especially for the children.

The insurgents went house to house, intimidating and bullying everyone they could possibly find, especially the Christians.

I told Kam to get his family and the children to safety as quickly as possible. I hung up the phone and immediately prayed, asking for direction and begging God to protect Kam and all the children I had hugged just weeks before—now their lives were at risk.

I made a few phone calls for help to friends in Kathmandu and within just a few hours, Kam loaded all 52 children on a public transport bus headed for the capital city.

We arranged to rent a house for them to stay in temporarily, hoping the threats and violence would soon blow over. It was a close call, but all were safe.

I met Kam eight years earlier in India. He was from Manipur, a northeastern state. He told me his story:

> "My mother died when I was only one year old. When I was older, I stopped going to school and began to earn money. I sold drugs and heroin every day. I myself became a drug addict. I was always afraid of the police. Every time I saw them, I thought they were coming to arrest me. I was constantly afraid of dying and going to hell. I couldn't sleep at night and I had no peace or joy.
>
> One day, there was a Bible Camp in our village. Someone shared the Gospel with me. The same night, I confessed my sins and accepted Jesus Christ as my Lord and personal Savior. I got joy and happiness. My fears were all gone. I wanted to know Him and learn His words, so I went to school for Bible training.
>
> After I completed my course, God gave me a vision to work with the poor people and take the Gospel to unreached places and I went to Nepal, near the border of Tibet."

Kam, a slight, dark-skinned man, rises early to begin his day.

He lives in the remote Nepalese village of Chaku, near the Tibetan border, not far from Mt. Everest. After several years of painstakingly slow ministry, he began a new church with more than 120 converts. He also started a Christian School with several hundred students, and a children's home with 52 disadvantaged and orphaned children. God was using this ministry in the middle of nowhere.

After ministering to his growing congregation in Chaku throughout the week, Kam treks through the towering Himalayan Mountains to share Christ in isolated villages where the Gospel has never been preached. Each day, he hikes for hours and sits under a tree to teach Nepali converts what it means to be a follower of Jesus Christ.

In Nepal, the Christians worship on Saturdays, so every week the villagers make their way to Chaku to worship with other believers.

Each Sunday afternoon, Kam boards an overcrowded, aging bus that strains and shudders through winding mountain roads taking him to Tibet. He rides for an hour and a half, then treks an hour by foot to reach a small village where he has led nine people to Christ. He spends the rest of the day ministering to this fledgling house church—one of the few known congregations of believers in all of Tibet. After a full day of ministry, Kam makes the long trek back to Chaku to begin another week.

After meeting and hearing Kam share about his ministry, I asked if I could help him by providing a building for them to worship in. A young college student who was traveling with me at the time overheard our conversation and later said, "I have money saved up for a new car. Would it be possible for me to use those funds to help him build a church building in Chaku?"

When we arrived back in the U.S., that young student sent a check for $4,000, and the building project for Kam's church began.

A year later, I visited Chaku for the first time. It took me all day to get there from Kathmandu. The road was washed out from the monsoons. We crossed rivers. We wound our way high into the towering mountains. We really were at "the top of the world."

When I saw that building for the first time, my eyes filled with tears, and when I met the new believers and heard their stories, I was sincerely touched. We sat on the floor of the church—the custom in Nepal—and worshipped God. It was truly an unforgettable experience.

Kam presented me with a traditional Nepali hat and a Manipuri shawl, a sign of respect and honor. That day, the village chief—who had donated the land for the building—and seven of his fellow villagers became Christ followers.

Until 1951, Nepal was totally closed to all outsiders. Bordered on the south by India and on the north by Tibet (China), its remote location and rugged terrain make it physically difficult to reach.

When the borders were finally opened to foreigners, there were no known Christians in Nepal . . . none! By 1960, it was estimated there were only 25 believers, but by 1985, there were 25,000. Today, it is estimated there are over 500,000 Christ followers in Nepal. Hundreds of church planters just like Kam are taking the Gospel where it has never gone before.

I think about that night, when I heard the distress in Kam's voice. After hanging up the phone, I thought about the children and couldn't sleep. I did all I could do at the time, and I knew it would be hours before I would hear if Kam and the children were safe. It was in God's hands.

Later, I called my good friend and World Help board member Skip Taylor and asked him for advice and help. He and his golfing buddies got together and raised emergency funds for the children's immediate care. In the weeks that followed, they also raised enough money to purchase a new children's home in Kathmandu.

Within a few months, we were all there to dedicate their new three-story building. The children sang songs and presented their cultural dances, thanking us over and over again for saving their lives.

As I looked into their faces, I wondered whether one of them would someday grow up to be another Kam.

CHAPTER TWENTY-TWO

weathering the storm

"SOMEDAY, WHEN IN THE PRESENCE OF OUR SAVIOR, WE WILL THANK HIM FOR EVERY BURDEN, EVERY TRIAL, AND EVERY HEARTACHE."

—J. VERNON McGEE[17]

W hat I had seen on television, as heart-wrenching as it was, didn't begin to prepare me for what I experienced in Southeast Asia. Everywhere we went, there were miles and miles of devastation. I have visited so many third-world countries; I thought I would be prepared for the horrendous conditions the reporters talked about. But I wasn't. Unimaginable destruction and the sights and smells of decomposing human bodies and rotting animal carcasses was more overwhelming than I'd ever imagined.

Although I was excited to be on the ground, meeting people face to face, the shock of actually being there was unbelievable — and it was just the beginning.

It was December 26, 2004, and almost immediately, everyone knew the Asian tsunami was one of the worst natural disasters in human history.

Our partners in the field sent us daily reports of what they witnessed firsthand and the tremendous challenges they faced while providing relief to the survivors. They found a few families housed in dilapidated school buildings, huddled together under plastic sheets, trying to stay warm. There were heartbreaking stories of hundreds of families with no food, shelter, or safe water to drink. They were helpless.

The devastation was so widespread that help did not arrive in many of the hardest-hit locations for days, and for some . . . weeks! The tsunami claimed at least 220,000 lives; the actual death toll will probably never be known.

In the province of Banda Aceh, Indonesia, our coworkers identified some 300 children under the age of 12 who became orphans after the tsunami. Many of the children watched as their parents were swept out to sea. Some wandered through the streets, while others huddled together in the airport with nowhere to go and no one to care for them. A plea was sent out to aid organizations to help these children.

Our Indonesian partners envisioned transporting the children to a Christian children's home in the capital city of Jakarta.

They told us, "We do not want to just distribute help and leave. We are committed to bringing help and hope to these children. To accomplish this means a long-term commitment."

Banda Aceh, the epicenter of the earthquake and tsunami, was totally annihilated. The Aceh people are strict Sunni Muslims who have been instrumental in spreading Islam throughout Indonesia and other parts of Southeast Asia. A common statement is, "To be Aceh is to be Muslim."

Normally, Banda Aceh is closed to foreigners and closed to the Gospel. But, because of this catastrophe, we were under the impression the government would allow any aid organization to rescue these stranded children.

As soon as we received this information, we sent an email out to all of our friends. We told them about the urgent need to get the children off the streets. It was a life-and-death issue; these children needed our help right away. Our friends responded immediately, and within a few short days we raised enough funds to begin helping some of these children. We were so excited, and it looked like the remaining funds would arrive soon.

Liberty University hosted a benefit basketball game. All the proceeds were designated for World Help's tsunami relief projects. During the game, Sky Angel television interviewed me and I shared the opportunity we had to make a difference and provide a future for these homeless and disadvantaged children.

Everything was coming together.

The next day, a reporter from the *Washington Post*—who somehow obtained my cell phone number—called me for an interview. He explained that he had read about our various relief projects from our website. He was particularly interested in the children's home project in Jakarta.

Two days later, the article appeared on the front page. It was nothing like he said it would be. The article was full of inaccuracies and implied that we were, in their words, "proselytizing helpless children." I was stunned. Why would anyone have a problem with us trying to help children?

The liberal media attempted to create the image that World Help was kidnapping children and indoctrinating them into Christianity. That was not even remotely accurate.

We simply saw children who were in dire need of immediate help. We wanted to rescue them by giving them food, shelter, clothing, an education, care, and love. We had the sincere desire to help them survive one of the most traumatic experiences of their young lives. We wanted to give them hope for the future.

Immediately, my phone started ringing. I received more than 100 requests for interviews in one day. I knew what they wanted—a controversy. But I decided not to grant any interviews in my state of mind at that time. Hopefully the story would go away.

That was hard for me. My nature is to confront and fight, especially when World Help is wrongly accused.

The next day a second article was on the front page of the *Washington Post,* and our partners informed us that the story had even been picked up by the *Indonesia Republika*, a leading radical Muslim newspaper. The government of Indonesia clarified that officials would not allow the children to be taken to Jakarata. At that point, we immediately stopped the fundraising efforts for the Indonesian orphaned children, and the appeals were removed from our website.

And because of threats from militant Muslims, our partners that we were trying to help were forced into hiding. Some of them even had to leave the country. We immediately shifted all our energies towards our partners' protection and safety.

By then, the *Washington Post* story was picked up by every major newspaper and media outlet around the world— CNN, Fox News, BBC, the Associated Press, and Reuters. Suddenly World Help became the poster child for "proselytizing children."

I had two options. I could address the false accusations head on, or I could remain completely silent. Sean Hannity invited me to come on his show and clear the air. I can't begin to tell you how tempting that was. However, for the safety of our partners in Indonesia, we decided to stay out of the media as much as possible.

Our staff prayed, I sought counsel from our Board of Directors, and I asked for guidance from some of my friends. We decided to send a press release to address the inaccuracies of the articles. The text was a short summary of the events that had taken place, and it ended with the following paragraph:

I make no apologies for the fact that World Help is a Christian organization. We have provided humanitarian aid all over the world for the past 13 years and not once have we done so with "strings attached." While it is our desire that "giving a cup of cold water" in the name of Jesus would earn us the right to be heard, our primary purpose was to simply provide immediate help to hurting children. What we are attempting to do in Indonesia by providing tsunami orphans with a Christian children's home is no different than Mother Teresa taking Hindu orphans and placing them in her Christian children's home in Calcutta . . . and she received a Nobel Peace Prize for doing so.

We continued to raise funds for tsunami relief projects in other countries; we just did it quietly. We were involved in providing tents for refugee camps, survival kits, food, medicine, and teams of grief counselors.

Amazingly, God gave us the opportunity to help another group of children orphaned by the tsunami. We identified 379 children in South Thailand who were affected by the disaster. The Thai government was more than willing to accept help, even from Christian organizations. Our donors allowed us to use the funds we had raised for the Indonesian orphans to help these Thai children instead. In fact, we raised enough for a children's home—providing food, staff salaries, rent, and vehicles for three years.

At that point, I decided it was time to personally visit the tsunami zone. I wanted to see the destruction for myself. We had already provided food, shelter, and humanitarian aid, but now we wanted to do more—we wanted to help them rebuild.

Our goal on the trip to South India and Thailand was to have hands-on involvement in the distribution of relief supplies, visit the villages where our partners were working, and let the survivors know we cared about them and wanted to help them.

In the first village we visited, I stood on a heap of bricks and rubble to get a better view of the area. The frail man next to me quietly and slowly said, "I found my 7-year-old boy under that pile of bricks. He was dead. I had to dig him out and bury him. It was one of the hardest things I ever had to do."

As we walked through another camp, I met a father who told me he was holding his two children by the hand when the giant wave hit. He couldn't hold onto them as the surging waters ripped them from his arms. The last word he heard them speak was, "Father!" Their bodies were never recovered.

I couldn't imagine what these fathers felt. More than one-third of the tsunami victims were children.

Our teams of psychiatrists and grief counselors treated many people like 28-year-old Meenakshi, whose four children—ages 4 to 12—were swept away by a wall of water in the fishing village of Nagapattinam, India. While other survivors clamored for the rice we brought, this guilt-ridden woman sat in the corner and stared vacantly toward the ocean. She asked repeatedly, "Why didn't God spare me even one?"

There were countless stories of grief just like these, all of them so painful to hear.

We met for hours with the leaders of the Bang Sak village in Phuket, Thailand, reviewing plans for rebuilding their homes. Their faces were a mix of excitement and disbelief that someone actually wanted to help them in such a tangible, long-term way—especially someone from halfway around the world. We were able to help them rebuild 20 houses. One of the biggest surprises for us was when we saw that the village chief had already set aside land for a church without us even asking.

The next day, we heard about a Muslim village north of Phuket that had been completely destroyed—entirely swept away. The survivors hadn't received any supplies since the initial drop four weeks earlier. They were totally forgotten. We quickly loaded a huge truck with food, gas stoves, and many other supplies, and drove over two hours to that forgotten village.

When we arrived, it seemed like everyone in the village came out to greet us with open arms. We found 78 devastated families with nothing but the clothes on their backs. The effects of not having food and supplies for weeks were evident—they were starving, and their faces were sunken in. They looked so fragile. The chief thanked us over and over again.

We unloaded the truck and distributed the aid. We told them we were Christians and we wanted to help them in the name of Jesus. Their faces were full of gratefulness, relief, and joy. They had been abandoned for weeks, but finally someone had brought help.

I wasn't just unloading a truck, I was meeting a tremendous need—a need for survival. What would have happened to these men, women, and children had we not taken the time to go to them?

I believe God had us there for that one forgotten village.

Later that day, I sat on the front porch of one of their makeshift houses and drank coffee with a Muslim cleric. We shared stories and he talked about what life was like before the tsunami—and what the future might hold.

I realized that in the face of so much pain and devastation, God provided healing and hope. A Christian and a Muslim who otherwise would have never crossed paths were talking, laughing, crying, and even praying together.

He had weathered his storms, and I had weathered mine.

CHAPTER TWENTY-THREE

i climbed mt. everest . . .
well . . .

149

"WHEN JESUS SAW HIS MINISTRY DRAWING HUGE CROWDS, HE CLIMBED A HILLSIDE. THOSE WHO WERE APPRENTICED TO HIM, THE COMMITTED, CLIMBED WITH HIM. ARRIVING AT A QUIET PLACE, HE SAT DOWN AND TAUGHT HIS CLIMBING COMPANIONS."

—MATTHEW 5:1-2, THE MESSAGE

I climbed Mt. Everest . . . well . . . not actually all the way to the top. But at least to base camp . . . well . . . I didn't actually climb all the way to base camp. But I was there—I went by helicopter.

I was only 6 years old, but I will never forget May 29, 1953. Two historic events happened that day. First, the coronation of Queen Elizabeth II took place at Westminster Abbey in London. But more importantly—to a young boy that is—Sir Edmund Hillary and Sherpa Tensing Norgay became the first humans to summit the world's tallest mountain, Mt. Everest, 29,035 feet above sea level. They accomplished something that day that had never been done before.

From that moment, I was hooked. The events of that day made an incredible impact on my life and created a lifelong obsession.

When I was in high school, we lived in Colorado. One

summer at camp, I climbed Horn Peak—nearly 14,000 feet tall. I felt like I was "king of the mountain."

So in 1997, when my friend John Mabray, his son Trimble, my son Josh, and I were in Kathmandu, Nepal, to train pastors and future church planters, I secretly hoped to see "Chomlungma"—that's what the locals call Everest.

We took our sons to allow them to experience God's work, but we also hoped they would someday develop our same passion for ministry. On our day off, we chartered a helicopter and flew for about an hour, high into the Himalayas.

We flew over some spectacular sights. Our first stop was the village of Lukla, where we dropped off the extra fuel for our descent. Then we headed straight for Everest.

When we reached 16,000 feet, the pilot landed in a small Sherpa village of farmers and yak herders. Josh and I got out because there was too much weight for all of us to go any higher. We waited for about 30 minutes while John and Trimble went on to base camp.

The air was so thin. I couldn't do much trekking, but we looked around the village and took lots of video and photos. When the chopper returned, it was our turn—I couldn't wait.

We weaved our way through the world's tallest mountain range, and there it was . . . Everest. What an extraordinary sight! We hovered over base camp and then flew up near the Khumbu Ice Fall.

The pilot landed at Kalipatar, a few hundred yards from base camp. "You can get out now," he said. The elevation was 17,900 feet—we were over three miles high. I asked the pilot if he could shut the engine down and take our photo, but he told me, "I can't. The air is so thin at this altitude I might not be able to get it started again, and if that happens, we'll all die in a few hours from altitude sickness."

I turned to Josh and said, "Don't ever tell your mother what you just heard."

I might as well have landed on the moon—that's how excited I was. As I stepped out of the helicopter, I joked with Josh, "That's one small step for man . . . one giant leap for mankind."

Even walking a few yards from the helicopter, I found it difficult to breathe. I quickly took Josh's photo and he took mine. It's one of my most treasured possessions. In fact, it's still the screensaver for my laptop . . . a daily reminder of my dream come true.

As we stared at the trio of giant mountain peaks—Everest, Nuptse, and Lhotse—I put my hands on Josh's shoulders and whispered in one ear, "Look what God created. Isn't He awesome? You are seeing what very few 11-year-old American boys have ever seen. Don't ever forget this moment as long as you live."

On the way back down, I asked the pilot if we could stop at the village of Thangboche where the world's highest Buddhist monastery is located, and where Tensing Norgay stopped on his historic mission to receive a blessing from the priest and monks. We entered the monastery, took off our shoes and were told not to talk to or disturb the monks who were chanting and praying. One monk blew a large, 20-foot horn; others burned incense. I sensed that Josh and Trimble were absorbing everything.

When we left the monastery, I asked one of the monks, "Is there a Christian church in the village?" He looked at me as if I were crazy and laughed. I thought to myself, "I guess that means no." This was one of Nepal's many unreached villages.

As we flew back to Kathmandu, coming off our "high," all I could think of were the hundreds of unreached villages below us. No one had ever told them that God loves them, that Jesus Christ died for them, that they could have peace with God and enjoy Him forever. They had never heard of Jesus.

Sometime before George Mallory's unsuccessful attempt to summit Everest, an eager journalist asked him, "Why do you want to climb Mt. Everest?" His response, "Because it's there."[18] I thought to myself, why do we need to reach these villages with the Gospel of Jesus Christ? "Because they are there."

When we met with our pastor friends the next day, John and I challenged them to take the Good News to every one of those isolated villages. They caught the vision.

Their leader, a former Buddhist whose father was a Buddhist priest, developed a strategy to plant hundreds of new churches in the remote villages of Nepal by bringing 100 of the brightest and best to Kathmandu for six months of intensive training. He and his team also translated 10 volumes of church-planting curriculum and planned to teach the students how to train other pastors and church planters. In many Nepali village house churches, the first literate man to become a believer is appointed pastor, because he's the only one who can read the Bible. But he has no training at all.

After the six months of training, each church planter would then take 10 volumes of curriculum into the five major regions of Nepal and find 10 other men to train for one year. At the end of their 18-month strategy, they hoped to have more than 1,000 trained church planters.

God enabled me to mobilize American believers to provide over one million dollars to construct modest church buildings for these new village churches.

At the end of 18 months, all 1,000 church planters were trained and more than 1,500 new house churches were established. We raised the resources to provide more than 300 new buildings—many of them in the Everest region.

Through the years, I've had the privilege to dedicate many of these small church buildings in the villages of Nepal. One day, we were high in the Everest region visiting churches when our Nepali partner said, "See that mountain over there? If you look closely, you can see the shiny tin roof of one of the churches you provided."

I immediately said, "Let's go see it." He laughed.

He told me it was a four-hour trek to get there, and for me it would be all day. I asked him how they ever got the building materials up that high. "They carried everything in on their backs," he said.

As I sat there, reflecting on all God had done—the hundreds of pastors trained, the hundreds of churches planted, the hundreds of remote villages reached with the Gospel, and the 300 Americans who provided those church buildings now filled with Christ followers and worshippers of God—I was humbled.

It all began the day I climbed Mt. Everest . . . well . . . almost.

CHAPTER TWENTY-FOUR

i still call it burma

"CHRISTIANS LET THREE-FOURTHS OF THE WORLD SLEEP . . . IGNORANT OF THE SIMPLE TRUTH THAT A SAVIOR DIED FOR THEM."

—ADONIRAM JUDSON[19]

David Yone Mo was once the leader of a violent, notorious street gang, a drug addict—a man with just days left to live.

He contracted viral hepatitis from using dirty heroin needles. The disease ravaged his body to the point that his doctor sent David's mother home to begin making funeral preparations.

His diagnosis—David would be dead within a week.

Before leaving, David's mother—a devout Christian—left a Bible under his pillow. Realizing that his death was imminent, he began reading.

As he read the words of Jesus to the dying thief on the cross, *"Today you will be with me in paradise,"* God broke through his hardened heart and David gave his life to Christ. He immediately felt God's healing power surge through his body. He knew God had saved him and healed him.

Because of God's intervention, David was discharged from the hospital within the week. He could not know the Lord had great plans for his drug-abused body.

After his miraculous transformation, David led his friends and former gang members to Christ. His life transition—leaving the wild drug scene and becoming a loving husband and father—was not easy. His family had lived in constant fear of him for years. Over and over again, God honored his newfound faith and testimony. Many of his former drug buddies entered God's Kingdom, one by one.

Soon they formed a new "gang"—the Myanmar Young Crusaders.

After the military crackdown in 1989, the government changed the name of their country to Myanmar, but I still call it Burma. Many countries throughout the world have never officially recognized the name change.

In this nation of over 45 million people, less than 5 percent of the population professes Christ.

The people of Burma are intensely religious. In a land filled with beautiful gold-covered temples, the people are oppressed by the darkness of false religion and the enslavement of drug abuse. It is estimated that two out of every three young people in Burma are drug addicts.

During my first visit, I had the opportunity to minister in the Mayangyaung leper colony located about 50 miles from Yangon, the capital city. We were only the second group of foreigners allowed to visit.

Approximately 100 Christian families are among the residents of this colony situated at the end of a nearly deserted road. It was established by the government in an attempt to isolate—some say forget—the more than 3,000 residents stricken with this dreaded disease.

I was totally overwhelmed by these mostly forgotten brothers and sisters in Christ who suffer terribly with this disease but love Christ with all their hearts.

We also were privileged to dedicate a church that was planted the previous year. It already had 125 members.

Perhaps the most important part of my trip was conducting an intensive leadership training conference for 150 Burmese pastors.

The conference was crucial in reaching Burma with the Gospel, because the government has declared that no foreign missionaries are allowed in their country. I realized that the work of evangelism and discipleship must be done by national pastors—or it will not be done at all.

Many of these pastors traveled for hours just to receive training in God's Word. They have a great desire to reach their people with the Gospel.

These courageous men face extreme persecution and danger every day. God is using them to break down the strongholds of Buddhism, Hinduism, and Islam, but not without danger to themselves and their families' lives.

Many pastors are persecuted by the government. Others are disowned by their families, or beaten and driven out of towns and villages where they try to establish a church.

Most of these pastors, if not all, have given up everything for the sake of the Gospel. They labor tirelessly in spite of persecution and hardship, but I have never heard even one of them complain.

I met one young pastor, a former drug addict who found he was infected with AIDS. He has endured numerous beatings, death threats, and endless persecution for planting three churches in Amar—a city without a Christian witness of any kind.

As we prayed together, the pastor's words brought tears to my eyes. He said, "God, my life is in Your hands. I know my days are numbered, but in the time I have left, I want to serve You."

I also met a 28-year-old man who studied Buddhist scripture for four years and served as a Buddhist monk for eight years.

Despite devotion to his religion, he felt empty. He tried his best to obey the laws of his false religion but fell short. He found no comfort in reincarnation and often wondered if there were more to life after death than an endless, repeating cycle.

He kept asking himself, "What will fill the void I have in my heart?"

He finally attended a Christian church in his monk's robes, looking for spiritual answers. He received a Burmese Bible and as he read these verses, he found the answers he sought. *"Come to me, all you who are weary and burdened, and I will give you rest"*[20] and *"Whoever lives and believes in me will never die."*[21]

This young man became a Christian, attended four years of Bible College, and is serving Christ today as a pastor in Burma.

I met him again a year later at our pastors' conference outside the city of Mandalay. He told me, "I have a heart for evangelism. I want to reach the Buddhists in Burma. I know how to witness to them because I was once a Buddhist priest."

The Myanmar Young Crusaders sponsor numerous evangelistic crusades each year. They have started 200 churches in the last 20 years. They also direct three Bible colleges, operate an orphanage where they care for more than 100 children, minister in a large leper colony, provide HIV/AIDS hospice care, and direct a drug rehabilitation program with a success rate of 80 percent. The key to success in their drug program is the requirement that participants read the Bible, attend daily prayer meetings, and attend Bible college classes. Many graduates of the program are now missionaries in Burma.

Although you could never tell from her humble and kind spirit, David's wife Kathy was the backbone of this great ministry. She played a vital role in its founding in 1974 and its tremendous growth and success over the years.

Kathy was a wonderful helpmate for David. Besides five children of their own, they were also "parents" to about 20 orphans who lived in their home. For 21 years, Kathy cooked three meals every day for as many as 100 orphans and students—preparing 300 pounds of rice a day. Kathy knew beyond a shadow of a doubt this was God's will for her life.

Kathy passed away on April 24, 1999 after 37 years of marriage—her struggle with cancer finally over. I received this email from David on the day she died:

> *"Kathy went home to be with her Lord this evening at 4:45 p.m. She was suffering so much that I couldn't bear to see her in pain. She told me to pray for her so that she could go ahead and share the wonderful things God is doing in Myanmar. Today, she wanted me to be at her bedside the whole day. I prayed for her and showed her the video tapes of the rallies and messages I had preached. I was at her bedside when she looked at me, called my name once, and then went away to be with her Lord."*

I've been to Burma many times, but I will always remember my visit to the church founded by one of the greatest missionaries of all time, Adoniram Judson, who lived and died more than 100 years ago.

Judson and his wife labored for more than two years in Burma before finding an opportunity to share Christ. After six long years, only one person came to Christ. Judson labored in Burma for nearly 40 years, and when he died in 1850, there were only 10 Burmese believers. Looking objectively at his ministry, many would consider Adoniram Judson a dismal failure. History has proven otherwise.

One of the greatest accomplishments of Judson's life was the translation of Scripture into the Burmese language. His painstaking work was so accurate it remains the translation of choice among Burmese Christians.

Judson traveled to Burma in 1812 as America's first foreign missionary. He persevered in his mission despite personal tragedy, government persecution, and discouraging results. He is hailed today as the "spiritual father" to Burmese believers.

David knew I collected Bibles from around the world, and as a parting gift after one of my trips, he gave me a Burmese Bible. I quickly thumbed through it but couldn't read a word. It was all in Burmese, except for the title page which was in English. It read, "Translated by A. Judson."

He asked if I knew who Adoniram Judson was. I quickly said, "Of course!"

David looked at me and said something I'll never forget. "When Adoniram Judson came to my country there were no Christians—none! Today," he said, "there are more than six million Christians in Burma, and every one of them, without exception, can trace their spiritual heritage back to one man, an American by the name of Adoniram Judson."

David was diagnosed with liver cancer in April 2002 and underwent treatment in Singapore. The doctors gave him a 50-50 chance of survival, yet he never lost hope.

"When I think about this dreaded disease, I feel I have no hope at all," he said, "but when I think of Jesus, I know I have all the hope in the world." After many months of courageous struggle, David lost his battle with cancer on August 24, 2003. God called one of my heroes home.

Today, when I remember David and Kathy, I like to think of them together in heaven, both healthy and happy now. I can't help but think they are having long, grateful conversations with their spiritual forefather, Adoniram Judson.

CHAPTER TWENTY-FIVE

you won't see this on the evening news

"EVERYONE WHO WANTS TO LIVE A GODLY LIFE IN CHRIST JESUS WILL BE PERSECUTED."

—II TIMOTHY 3:12

O ur outlook on certain things can be influenced by what we see and hear from the media. Whether wrong or right, we form a preconceived idea.

But, if you're like me, you like to see things for yourself.

I tried several times to get into Iraq, but every time I made plans to go, there was either another kidnapping or a bombing, and travel was always highly discouraged, especially by my wife.

Instead, we went to Cairo, Egypt, and met our Egyptian "Bibles for Iraq" project director.

The director had just returned from a week in Iraq where he coordinated the distribution process for the Bibles World Help provided. He told me that terrorists targeted our team's convoy with gunfire. We were thankful no one was hit, but it was a close call. He also said the recent terrorist violence significantly increased the danger to those who are willing to risk their lives to get God's Word into the hands of our Christian brothers and sisters in Iraq.

A Christian leader, working behind the scenes and underground in Egypt to help with the church-planting efforts in the Middle East, told me he had been beaten, imprisoned, and even hung upside down and tortured because of his faith.

In Iraq—and in all of the Arabic-speaking Muslim countries—when Muslims convert to Christianity, they are disowned by their families. All ties are broken. Sometimes family members even call the police. According to Islamic law, converts to Christianity have 30 days to "come back to their senses and back to Islam." After the 30 days, if they have not returned to Islam, they can legally be killed. Some new Christians don't even tell anyone they are believers. Most have to leave home and family, move to a new city, and start a new life.

It was a very instrumental meeting, but as I left Egypt, I couldn't help but feel a little disappointed. I hadn't been able to visit Iraq or meet any Iraqi pastors.

I arrived back in New York on a Saturday afternoon and immediately caught a plane for Minnesota to speak the next morning to more than 6,000 people at Grace Church in Eden Prairie. Just before I was to speak, the worship leader said, "We will have a very special guest speaker tonight, a pastor of one of the largest evangelical churches in Iraq. His church has an attendance of 1,500 on any given Sunday morning with hundreds of Muslim seekers."

I couldn't believe it! I had just returned from the Middle East where I couldn't get into Iraq, and here I was in the U.S., sitting in a church, and this Iraqi pastor was just a few feet from me.

Between the two morning services, I introduced myself to him (his identity needs to remain secret for security reasons) and we ducked into a side room to talk. He shared his stories of what God was doing in Iraq. He said he recently put a sign up in front of the church in Arabic saying, "Jesus is the Light of the World"— the first Christian sign or billboard in Baghdad. A few days later, some militant Shiite Muslims put up a cardboard sign in front of the church that said, "Jesus is not the Light of the World . . . Mohammed is the Light of the World and we are warning you."

He responded by giving his Muslim neighbors much-needed medicine and gifts. He asked them if they respected the Bible and Jesus as a prophet. When they said, "Yes," he gave them all New Testaments and turned to John 8:12, where Jesus said, *"I am the light of the world."* Amazingly, these militant Muslims said, "We are sorry. We respect you and want to be your friends."

God uses this courageous pastor to build bridges in his war-torn nation. He spends one day each week discipling pastors and Christian leaders in a training center in Baghdad.

I told him about World Help and our Bible project—he already knew about it. He told me many people had received the Bibles and were reading, studying, and wanting to know more about Jesus Christ.

We prayed together, and a great friendship and partnership began. It was truly a God-directed beginning.

I told him I wanted to visit Iraq, but he highly discouraged it as well. It was just too dangerous at that time, so once again, I had to wait. I think God was trying to teach me patience.

During my next trip to the Middle East, and as a result of my meeting with our new Iraqi partner, many Iraqi pastors and friends were able to meet with us in Amman and Cairo. We spent time in prayer, talking over our strategy to complete the "Bibles for Iraq" project, and planning for future projects while there was a window of opportunity.

We learned there are as many as three million Iraqi refugees in the country of Syria alone—and millions more throughout the Middle East—who were forced to leave their homes and families behind. They have nothing. More than 750,000 Iraqi children died over a period of a few years because of sanctions and lack of medicine.

We met with many of these refugees who gathered together for prayer and worship. We didn't see despair and hopelessness.

Instead, we saw smiling faces and heard children singing. I realized only God could give these hurting people such joy in their circumstances.

We worshipped together with these displaced brothers and sisters and shared words of encouragement. We prayed for them, their country and their families back home in Iraq. It was an extremely emotional moment.

We also provided food, clothing, medicines, blankets, and even electric heaters to the refugees—just to help them survive and get through the winter.

Our partner explained that because of the recent bombings near his church in Baghdad, he and members of his congregation have to sleep in the church building each night and stand guard 24 hours a day. Every time a car approaches he holds his breath. But once it passes, he thanks God for giving them their lives back again. He said that every morning before their children leave for school, they pray they will be able to see them again in the afternoon.

I was amazed by his courage and inspired by his unwillingness to compromise or give in to his fears.

Another Iraqi pastor told me that the persecution against Christians was increasing. Recently, two young Christian girls were kidnapped, raped, murdered, and their mutilated bodies were dumped on the steps of the church.

Churches have been threatened. If they ring their bells, the insurgents will bomb them. The extremists tell the Iraqi people not to buy anything, especially land, from Christians. The extremists' goal is to kill all Christians or drive them out of Iraq. When they're gone, the extremists will confiscate their land for free.

One pastor shared that insurgents painted a sign on the side of his church that said, "Convert to Islam or be killed." I realized

Iraq not only needed political liberation from the tyranny of Saddam Hussein, but they urgently needed spiritual liberation from the tyranny of Satan.

Our team visited a mosque in downtown Cairo in the middle of the day. There were at least 10,000 people praying. Five thousand were on their knees inside the building, and thousands more were outside, blocking the sidewalks and streets.

I heard their prayers and the cleric's midday sermon blaring over a loud speaker. The Muslims knelt with their faces to the ground for nearly an hour. Nearby were hundreds of armed riot police with helmets, shields, and tear gas. They feared a protest might break out because of the growing tension throughout the Middle East. We stood in the midst of thousands of Muslims—praying with our eyes open—asking God to open their spiritual eyes.

It dawned on me that this was not only happening at that mosque, but also in thousands of mosques throughout Cairo, a city of 18 million people. Hundreds of millions of Muslims were praying at that same moment all around the world.

In spite of years of tyranny, war, and insurgency, God has allowed World Help to make a significant impact in Iraq and the entire Middle East. Our ministry has provided nearly one million Bibles for new believers, a Christian student center across the street from Baghdad University where some 50,000 students attend, church buildings, a children's center, and discipleship training for the hundreds of new believers in Iraq. It is truly amazing to see what God is doing to build His Kingdom in the Middle East.

The Spirit of God is moving with undeniable power in Iraq and the Church has discovered a newfound spiritual freedom. That's something you won't see on the evening news.

CHAPTER TWENTY-SIX

poppy, have you ever
been to nineveh

"UNLESS THERE IS AN ELEMENT OF RISK IN YOUR EXPLOITS FOR GOD, THERE IS NO NEED FOR FAITH."

—J. HUDSON TAYLOR[22]

I was spending a day in the park with my 7-year-old grandson Riley when out of the blue he asked me, "Poppy, have you ever been to Nineveh?"

It didn't take me long to realize that he had just learned about the story of "Jonah and the Whale" in Sunday school. "No," I told Riley, "but I'm about to go in a few weeks."

After several failed attempts to enter Iraq, this time we were actually going in.

The destruction, threats, bombings, and military presence were reported nightly on the news, but there was another side of the coin—humanity, the Iraqi people. Did Iraqis really hate Americans as depicted in the news or were they grateful to us? Did they want Americans to stay and help them get established in the new government or were they anxious to get us out of their country?

I was about to find out for myself as our World Help team embarked on one of the most incredible missions experiences of my life. Anxious, excited, and maybe a little fearful, we trusted God to have us in the right place at the right time and with the right people. We knew nothing would happen to us by accident; our lives were in His hands.

Our ministry partner in Iraq helped us coordinate this mission and our meetings. He and his family flew from Baghdad to Amman, Jordan, to meet and travel with us for added security. But while they were in the Baghdad airport, terrorists exploded a car bomb nearby. All flights were cancelled and the airport was closed. Our partner, his wife, and their three small children were forced to sit in the airport for nearly 24 hours.

When they finally joined us in Amman, he quickly changed our tickets and re-routed us to another city. Arriving in Iraq, we discovered that terrorists had attacked again not far from us, near the Old Testament city of Nineveh. Several explosions killed many and the roads were closed. American soldiers were sent in to stabilize the situation.

It was one thing to hear stories of terrorism on television; it was entirely another thing to witness them myself.

On our first day, I met with some government officials who shared their personal stories of torture and oppression. In one day, they said Saddam Hussein had murdered—with weapons of mass destruction—more than 180,000 of his own people from that area.

We visited one of the villages that Saddam destroyed—a place where over 5,000 Iraqis are trying to rebuild. We distributed humanitarian aid supplies and gave *Christmas for an Orphan* boxes to the children. We shared lots of smiles, hugs, and even a few tears.

Our team visited a new church building under construction. Its young congregation already had more than 300 Muslim converts. I only know of a few churches in all of the Middle East with that many former Muslims.

When Saddam was in power, there were only five evangelical churches in all of Iraq. Now there are 12 new churches in the city of Baghdad alone, and hundreds throughout the country.

One of the highlights of our trip was a three-day leadership training conference with over 250 pastors and Christian leaders. Many of them drove hundreds of miles out of the way because of blocked roads from recent terrorist attacks. There were delegates from Baghdad, Kirkuk, Basra, Erbil, and Mosul (Nineveh), as well as from cities in Iran and Turkey—truly an international conference.

Many of the leaders had suffered persecution and imprisonment under Saddam. Others were victims of insurgents and terrorists. One elder of a church in Baghdad told me that only a few months earlier their pastor, his wife, and their son were kidnapped and they haven't been heard from since. Visibly shaken, he told me, "We hope and pray they are still alive."

These Iraqi pastors and leaders were passionate in their worship of God. Every night, for more than an hour, they waved banners, raised their hands to the heavens and sang songs of spiritual victory. It was one of the most amazing worship experiences of my life.

I had the opportunity to teach a session on how to face persecution and adversity, but I felt so inadequate as I faced these brave men and women who have gone through so much more than I could ever imagine. I shared my own struggles with cancer and at the close of the session, many of them wept and prayed for each other.

On the final day of the training, John Lloyd taught about forgiveness. It was a time of spiritual healing for all of us. My Iraqi brothers and sisters admitted, "We have much to forgive."

That night, as our three days of intensive training came to a close, we invited all of the pastors to come forward and sit in front of the people. We asked if it would be possible for us, as Americans, to humbly wash their feet as a sign of servant leadership. Just imagine the emotions that swept over us as we knelt before these courageous Iraqi brothers and sisters.

When we tried to leave Iraq via Baghdad, our plane was turned back en route and forced to land in the city of Sulaimaniyah in Northern Iraq.

Our team was disappointed until we later found out the lawyer for Saddam was assaulted in the Baghdad airport. This created quite a disturbance. For security reasons, airspace in and out of Baghdad was closed, as well as the airport.

When we finally landed in Sulaimaniyah, we were emotionally and physically tired. To top that off, there were no hotel rooms available. We had to spend the night in an apartment with no heat or electricity—which made for a cold night.

After a 24-hour delay, we finally arrived in Baghdad. As we landed, I looked out over the city at the destruction left by the war. I saw the former palace of Saddam Hussein—a vivid reminder of his evil power. As we stepped off the plane, we felt the presence of our U.S. military all around the airport. There were hundreds of armed security guards. Everyone was tense and on edge because of Saddam's trial, and the Iraqi elections were only a few days away. History was unfolding in Baghdad.

We were so close to the action, but because of high security, we were not allowed to leave the airport to visit our partner's church. It was considered too dangerous. But God was once again protecting us.

Our partner called on his cell phone to tell us he had arrived back home safely, but bombs were exploding all around his neighborhood and the walls of his house were shaking. He said there were many U.S. military helicopters in the air and reports of several other incidences throughout the city. It really is a war zone and we could have been right in the middle of it.

With all the difficulties and obstacles we experienced getting in and out of Iraq, I realized how fortunate we are to live in America, a free country.

Coming home, I was able to tell my grandson about my visit to Nineveh—a place that needed God thousands of years ago and still needs Him today.

CHAPTER TWENTY-SEVEN

thank you for bringing the mission field to our church

"SILENT NIGHT, HOLY NIGHT. ALL IS CALM, ALL IS BRIGHT."

—JOSEPH MOHR[23]

I walked down the dark hallway holding only a candle to light my way. The electricity had gone out in the old Indian guest house where I was staying in Chennai, India. I was bored and decided to joke around with my brother-in-law Daniel Henderson who was staying in another room down the hall. As I slowly made my way to his room in the dark, I sang "Silent Night" and pretended to Christmas carol outside his door. It was March!

Daniel, who is now the president of Strategic Renewal International (SRI), was with me in India to train leaders and church planters.

After a few laughs, we sat down for some small talk until the electricity came back on. A few minutes into that conversation, Daniel said, "Hey Vernon, I've been meaning to tell you something. A children's choir from Africa recently came to our church, and when they were done singing, there wasn't a dry eye in the place. I thought of you and all the countries where you work. You should have a choir of children from all over the world. You could call it 'Children of the World.'"

Have you ever had one of those moments where things just click inside your head? Some would call it an "Ah-ha!" moment.

I had one. Daniel could barely get the words out of his mouth before my mind started racing. Only a few weeks earlier, while sitting in a staff meeting at World Help, we tried to figure out how we could have one of the children we had helped in another country travel with us and give their personal testimony in our presentations. This was the answer—only better.

As soon as I returned from that trip, I immediately worked to make the vision of this choir a reality. I knew that if God was in that vision, He would provide the leadership, children, and schedule.

Within a few days, my daughter Nikki said she would help lead the first team. She was engaged to be married at the time and made the decision before even talking to her fiancé. Thankfully, Mark was just as excited to work with the team as Nikki was. So, we had the leadership; now we just needed the children. This was no easy task. Not only did we want to find children who we could help, but also there were government regulations, U.S. requirements, visas, health exams, vaccinations, and much more.

Our partnership in India with a ministry that had an orphanage in Manipur had just begun. On my first visit, I found several hundred needy children living in dilapidated buildings and sleeping on mud floors. There were overgrown trees and shrubs, scant resources, and snakes. I hate snakes!

These children had lost their parents due to tribal warfare and preventable diseases. Some were abandoned because their parents simply could not afford to take care of them. The home is called "Gilgal Children's Home," and I could not think of a more appropriate name. In Joshua, this same name is mentioned: "*Then the Lord said to Joshua, 'As slaves in Egypt you were ashamed, but today I have removed that shame.' So Joshua named that place Gilgal, which it is still named today.*"[24] In India, as in many countries, being an orphan or abandoned brings about unbelievable shame for these young children; but at Gilgal, all shame is removed. The children enjoy a place of hope in spite of their pain.

I immediately bonded with the director of the home, James Lalrubal, or "Big Daddy," as the children affectionately call him. Over the years, I have visited Gilgal at least 10 times, and James has become one of my best friends. He genuinely loves and cares for these children day in and day out.

At the time, the home's limited funds could not provide the nutritious food, medical attention, and educational opportunities these children needed. It's not that the staff didn't love the children; they just didn't have the resources to care for them. That day, I promised James and the children we would help them. I wasn't sure how, but I knew we had to help.

In the fall of 2000, *Children of the World* was born. Our first choir was made up of 20 children: 12 from Gilgal, 2 from Burma, 3 from Nepal, and 3 from the Philippines.

The choir traveled across the U.S. for 10 months of the year, performing in churches, schools, and conferences. The choir's mission was to raise awareness of the plight of disadvantaged and orphaned children around the world. The leaders also encouraged people to reach out and sponsor a child in need. My daughter and new son-in-law spent their honeymoon and first year of marriage on the road with these special children. Whenever I introduced them in a concert, I would say, "They've only been married three months and already have 20 children!"

Looking back over these nine years of *Children of the World*, it's hard to believe all that the choirs have accomplished, performing in such venues as the Crystal Cathedral, which is televised in over 200 countries, the Brooklyn Tabernacle, Liberty University, Willow Creek Community Church, and Shadow

Mountain Community Church with David Jeremiah. They have also performed and recorded with musical artists Mike Tait, Steven Curtis Chapman, and Richie McDonald of Lonestar.

But more importantly, World Help has invested in the lives of 290 needy children who have come to the U.S. to be part of these choirs. Because of their efforts, we have seen more than 31,000 sponsorships for children in need and thousands of dollars raised to repair and build children's homes around the world.

We kept our promise to Gilgal—they now have a new school, several new dorms, a church building, improved food, and medical treatment.

But the highlight of the choir's first tour was at a concert in Nashville, Tennessee. I sat on the front row with the pastor while the children were singing. He leaned over to me and said, "Thank you for bringing the mission field to our church."

Who would have thought that a moment of singing "Silent Night" in a pitch black hallway in India would become such a major ministry of World Help and such a *defining moment* of my life.

CHAPTER TWENTY-EIGHT

hungry . . . hopeless . . .
running for their lives

"IF YOU CAN ACCOMPLISH ONLY ONE THING TODAY, TOMORROW, OR IN YOUR LIFETIME . . . LET IT BE THAT YOU SAVE THE LIFE OF A CHILD."

—VERNON BREWER

As I looked at her, I saw a mere child—shaking and sobbing. Grace had experienced more pain in her 13 brief years than I had in my entire life. I didn't know what to do or say; I was shocked by her story. I longed to take her in my arms—like I would one of my own daughters—and tell her it would be okay. But she wasn't done telling me her story, and I knew she needed to get it all out.

Grace was born in a remote village in Northern Uganda. She lived in a small hut with her family and grew up like most of the children in the area. She loved her mother and father and they were all very happy . . . until one dark night that changed her life forever.

Grace was abducted by the Ugandan Lord's Resistance Army (LRA) when she was just a child. The rebel soldiers stormed into their small home, killed her father and beat her mother. They dragged Grace out of the hut and threatened to kill her if she did not do as she was told.

The rebels forced her to carry a weapon and ammunition for the army. She was raped repeatedly and became pregnant by one of the soldiers. She became a child mother when she was only 12 years old. Then, tragically, Grace was forced to watch while the soldiers shot her baby.

After they killed her baby, Grace tried to escape but was captured and severely beaten—more than 100 lashes. When she recovered, and in spite of dangerous circumstances, Grace finally managed to escape.

I couldn't believe what I was hearing. I tried to reach out to her as best I could—to somehow comfort her. I wanted her to know I cared about her and wanted to help her. Memories of Grace and her tragic story will always haunt me.

But she's not the only one. At the height of the rebel attacks, every night, more than 40,000 children, some as young as 5 years old, would leave their villages to take refuge in the towns of Northern Uganda, then make the trek home the next morning. Parents didn't know if their children would make it home safely the next day, and children didn't know if their parents would be there when they returned home.

Some nights as many as 14,000 of these children would find safety in the town of Gulu. These boys and girls carried only a mat for sleeping. They walked as far as eight miles to escape abduction, rape, and violent attacks by the Ugandan rebels. The fortunate ones found places to sleep in courtyards or churches, but most of these children ended up sleeping on the streets. But even that was better than the alternative!

These are Uganda's "Forgotten Children."

Can you imagine thousands of children walking into your city or town every night at dusk? Many of them aren't able to attend school, and those who do are forced to do their homework in the dark. They have no jobs, no place to live, nowhere to sleep, nothing to eat—and no one to care for them and protect them. Many say it would be better to be dead than to live the way they are living.

Carol Bellamy, former executive director of UNICEF, described the desperate need. "The world needs to wake up to the enormity of the crisis in Northern Uganda." she said. "This is one of the most serious humanitarian emergencies in the world."[25]

Because the majority of the violence is focused in Uganda and the Sudan, most people don't know the LRA is one of the largest terrorist organizations in the world. Joseph Kony, their ruthless leader, practices a cocktail of Christianity, Islam, and witchcraft. He claims that the Holy Spirit directs his military initiatives.

Kony tells members of his young, cult-like army to cover their skin with oil so spirits will protect them when they go into battle. If they are worthy and without sin, the bullets are supposed to bounce off them. If they are killed, Kony reasons that the young "soldiers" must have secret sins in their lives and deserve to die.

The LRA preys on children because they're easily influenced. As soon as children are abducted, many are forced to kill their own family—brothers, sisters, mothers, and fathers. The LRA's goal is to instill so much shame and guilt into these young boys and girls that they feel they can never go home again. And for the most part, it works.

Children who refuse, or those who cannot keep up with the rest of the rebels, are killed on the spot. Complaining, expressing sorrow or guilt, or not following commands are all grounds for instant death. Any child caught trying to escape is brought back to the other "child soldiers" who are forced to brutally kill the "deserter." Anything becomes a weapon—knives, sticks, clubs, rocks, bare hands—anything.

Our partner in Uganda, Alex Mitala, is the leader of a denomination of 10,000 churches spread throughout the country. We have worked with his Good Samaritan Children's

Home in Kampala for more than five years. After we expressed our desire to do something to help the Forgotten Children, we chartered a plane and flew to Gulu where this unbelievable tragedy unfolded.

I was not prepared for what I saw in Gulu, even though I had heard about the crisis. But to see it with my own eyes—was indescribable.

I met hundreds of Forgotten Children just like Grace. Those who were captured but managed to escape live in constant fear of being abducted again. Countless young girls are infected with HIV/AIDS by rebel soldiers and many have become child mothers.

The children's terrifying nightmares continue; they couldn't even tell me their stories without breaking down—their bodies shaking with sobs.

A young boy named Moses described his ordeal. "One night, the rebel soldiers barged into our hut, began beating everyone, and dragged us out into the open," he said.

He watched as they clubbed his mother and father over and over again. They took Moses and his brother away. He was terrified because he had heard about other children who were kidnapped, but he was relieved that at least he wasn't alone. His brother was with him. But that instant of relief quickly disappeared.

The rebels suddenly stopped by a small stream and turned to the boys. They put a gun to Moses's head and told him to kill his brother or they would kill him.

Moses told me he cried and kept saying that he couldn't do it, but the soldiers screamed at him and pushed the end of the gun hard into his head. His brother yelled over and over, "Do it . . . you will live . . . do it!"

Before he had time to think, Moses pulled the trigger. His

185

brother lay sprawled in the dirt—unmoving with blood running from his chest.

Moses was visibly shaken as he recounted his tragic story. I gently told him God understood and would forgive him. It wasn't his fault.

The more children I met and stories I heard, the more I knew that God brought me to this place, at this particular time, for a specific purpose. I knew He wanted World Help to do something significant to help these suffering Forgotten Children.

But, there are so many children, so many horrific stories and so much that must be done. Where do you start?

One night, we visited a site called Noah's Ark where several hundred of the Forgotten Children slept in tents. Nearly 4,000 slept in Gulu that particular night. Some slept at a government-safe compound, some on the floor of a bus park, and some out in the open.

I stood next to our ministry partner as we watched more than 300 children as they sang, praised God, and prayed. I looked at Alex, who was weeping. "These atrocities must stop!" he cried. It was difficult for either of us to speak.

I asked for permission to stay and spend more time with the children. As I tucked those young boys in and prayed with them, I knew I would never forget these Forgotten Children as long as I live.

A pastor in Northern Uganda said, "We want to help them, but our people are so poor. We have the compassion, we just don't have the money."

I prayed, asking God for a culturally sensitive plan that would allow those pastors to meet this great need. I wasn't interested in making our presence known or getting credit for anything we would do. I simply wanted to provide the resources these pastors needed so they could take care of these children.

The pastors developed a simple, effective strategy. They identified 10 churches in Northern Uganda whose buildings were only used a few hours each week. These buildings would house much-needed Good Samaritan Children's Centers. Each church would choose 50 of the neediest children to be helped. The pastor and his wife would serve as the directors and coordinators for that particular center. All funds would help to provide food, clothing, medicine, and educational assistance, as well as trauma and grief counseling.

Each center would cost $39,000 for one year. Our immediate goal was to raise $390,000 to get all 10 centers up and running. I asked Alex to gather the pastors together so we could pray about this great need. They arrived from all over Northern Uganda. When we all sat down, and I looked into their faces, I knew there was no way I could send them home empty-handed. They all had a strong compassion for these children. They were sacrificing their time out of love.

We could not possibly wait another year to help these children—we had to act immediately.

I told these pastors, "We don't have the money, but I will go home and cast the vision for these Forgotten Children. Somehow, by faith, in the next 60 days we will trust God to meet this need."

"Our job is to work hard and cast the vision," I said. "Your role in this partnership is to pray."

And did those pastors ever pray! When we finished praying, I didn't know how we would do it, but I knew God would make it happen.

Within days of returning home, God began to answer our prayers. Through many compassionate and generous friends, we raised enough money to start all 10 centers. It didn't take 60 days . . . it only took six!

I realized the power of those Ugandan pastors' prayers and

that God was honoring our joint partnership efforts to help the Forgotten Children.

The story of the Forgotten Children is definitely tragic, but there is hope in the midst of despair. World Help is currently funding 12 children's centers, including a vocational school and sports outreach, impacting a total of 4,000 children.

I am sure you will agree with me that when we stand before God, we want to be able to say, "I did something."

"One day a man was walking along the beach when he noticed a figure in the distance. As he got closer, he realized the figure was that of a boy picking something up and gently throwing it into the ocean. Approaching the boy he asked, 'What are you doing?'

The youth replied, 'Throwing the starfish back into the ocean. The sun is up and the tide is going out. If I don't throw them back, they'll die.'

'Son,' the man said, 'don't you realize there are miles and miles of beach and hundreds of starfish? You can't possibly make a difference.'

After listening politely, the boy bent down, picked up another starfish, and threw it into the surf. Then smiling at the man, he said, 'I made a difference for that one.'"[26]

i did not make myself an orphan

"BEFORE THE DEATH OF OUR PARENTS, WE WERE HAPPY. DAD AND MOM USED TO TAKE GOOD CARE OF US. WE HAD A REAL GOOD LIFE. AFTER THEIR DEATH, WE GOT SCATTERED AND STARTED TO SUFFER."

—AUGUSTINE, 9-YEAR-OLD AIDS ORPHAN

"There are three [children] in all," she said. "They are all infected. The mother is infected. These kids are suffering. There's nothing at all. They've got no clothing. They've got no food. There's no income at home, because the mother is sick. No one is helping them."

Because the traumatized little girl didn't talk much, the kind lady who found Nozake told me her story. As I listened, I almost felt guilty for my life, my own health, and that of my family.

Nozake walked up shyly and never looked me in the eyes. This quiet 10-year-old was one of hundreds of children we met just outside Markman Township, South Africa. All the women and children who crowded in and around the small, dust-filled concrete compound are affected by AIDS. All are extremely poor, and most have been abandoned.

As we talked with Nozake and the others, I thought about how foreign their circumstances seemed to me. These children know nothing but extreme poverty. Every meal is a struggle.

School is a privilege, not an assumption. Suffering is a daily part of life. Many of them have never lived a day without the effects of AIDS.

I soon learned the reason for Nozake's withdrawn demeanor; this little girl was raped by her mother's boyfriend. The "monster" infected her with HIV. When I heard about the torture this child was forced to endure in her own home, I knew her pain ran deeper than the disease that invaded her little body. Nozake's spirit was crushed.

I could only imagine how she must live in fear and shame. How was she supposed to trust anyone ever again? She had not been violated by a stranger, but by someone her mother allowed into her life.

As I fought back the tears, I hugged Nozake and wished I could take her pain away. I knew I would never forget her.

Nozake and her family are among millions who are living with the pain and impact of AIDS and its daily, never-ending toll.

Those of us who are fortunate to live in a nation not completely engulfed by AIDS sometimes have a hard time understanding or relating to those who live in its presence every day. After meeting child after child like Nozake, I thought, "What a different world from mine."

But then something happened that changed my mind and heart.

A railroad track ran near the building where we were meeting. Right in the middle of our visit, we could hear the deep rumble and piercing horn of an approaching train. Boys from across the compound began running to the fence. They lined up with excitement, hooking their fingers into the chain link fence and watching the mighty train rush past. They laughed and gestured with glee as it roared by. Their excitement brought a smile to my face as I remembered the same reaction to trains from my own children and grandchildren. Boys will be boys—no matter if they were born in Lynchburg, Virginia, or Markman Township, South Africa. And boys like trains.

As I watched them, I saw these children for who they were, children just like my own. They are boys and girls like those we love. They feel, love, and hurt—just like you and me. The only difference is, their families and communities are living with a plague that devours all they hold dear.

AIDS will cause more deaths than any other epidemic disease in history. It is the biggest public health problem the world has ever faced. It already surpasses the bubonic plague, which wiped out 25 million people—one quarter of Europe's population at the time.[27]

Every 10 seconds, one person dies of AIDS and another two are infected. A total of three million people die each year from AIDS. This staggering number has been compared to 20 fully loaded 747s crashing every single day for an entire year.[28]

Of the 42 million people living with HIV/AIDS, 70 percent are in sub-Saharan Africa.[29] In some African countries, more than one-third of the population is infected.

As always, it is the children who suffer the most. Over fifteen million have been orphaned by AIDS,[30] a number which is expected to increase to 40 million by 2010.[31] Every 14 seconds, a child is orphaned by AIDS in Africa.[32]

Without parents or older family members to raise them, most of these children end up on the streets. They become a high-risk group for AIDS themselves, plus sexual exploitation and abduction. They live with no hope of a better future.

Despite these overwhelming statistics, American Christians are relatively apathetic to the growing HIV/AIDS crisis. A recent Barna report shows that only 14 percent of born-again Christians said they would help HIV/AIDS orphans overseas.

Only 14 percent![33]

I have a confession to make. A few years ago, I was ignorant about the scope and devastation of HIV/AIDS. I knew people were dying in Africa and we were doing our best to help needy children there, but I'm ashamed to admit I did not know all the facts—the extent of the devastation HIV/AIDS has caused in Africa in so many ways. It's not that I didn't have compassion. I just didn't know. Now I do. I've seen the pain and suffering firsthand.

I first came face to face with the heartbreaking tragedy of AIDS in 1987. I was on a mission trip to Uganda. The devastation was just beginning. Before then, I only saw news footage or read about the epidemic that was spreading its death grip across the world.

Since then, I have seen the face of AIDS in one form or another through the global work of World Help. The orphans, the hungry, the poverty-stricken, the war victims—AIDS is both a contributing factor to and a product of many of these situations.

God has placed a tremendous burden on my heart and the heart of every staff member at World Help for the children affected by AIDS, children who are abandoned and orphaned because of this tragic pandemic.

Many Christians still believe that AIDS is a disease of homosexuals, prostitutes, and drug users. Some think it is a curse from God for sin. We, especially as Christians, have been slow to respond. Why? Stigma, indifference, apathy, racial prejudice— perhaps all of these have paralyzed the Church of Jesus Christ today.

Recently, after I finished speaking at a church in southern California, the pastor stood and said, "Some think the life of a black-skinned, brown-eyed child in Africa is not as important as the life of a white-skinned, blue-eyed child in America. Shame on us!"

Perhaps because we have forgotten that we serve a God whose Son exemplified compassion. Jesus did not care how a person became ill or why they were suffering. He didn't ask if they had done something wrong that caused their suffering. He simply reached out, touched them, and healed them.

Leprosy was the AIDS of Jesus' day, and yet, Jesus—the ultimate advocate and example of compassion—reached out and touched lepers. "Jesus reached out His hand and touched the eyes of the blind, the skin of the person with leprosy, and the legs of the cripple . . . Jesus knew love usually involved touching."[34]

I recently visited the Kigali Memorial Centre in Rwanda where thousands of victims of the 1994 genocide are buried. As I walked through the memorial, I saw pictures of men, women, boys, and girls who had been killed in the genocide. Listed were their names, ages, and how they were killed. It was unimaginable. As I looked at these images, one particular quote pierced my heart: "I did not make myself an orphan." The author was listed only as an unknown child affected by the genocide in Rwanda, but the child could have easily been Nozake or any of the other 15 million children who are orphaned by AIDS.

The ones who are suffering the most are the children. They are innocent. What we do will affect them more than anyone else.

Bono, a rock star and lead singer of the group U2, may be doing more to address the AIDS crisis than any other single person in the world. When addressing a group of Christians in Washington, Bono said, "There is a continent—Africa—being consumed by flames. I truly believe that when the history books are written, our age will be remembered for three things: the war on terror, the digital revolution, and what we did—or did not do—to put out the fire in Africa. History, like God, is watching what we do."[35]

I've committed the rest of my life to be a Voice of Hope. I want to be an advocate for the children orphaned by HIV/AIDS. My prayer is that Christians will not turn away. May the historians and history books say that when the AIDS pandemic was at its height, it was the Church of Jesus Christ that got involved; it was Christians who had compassion.

CHAPTER THIRTY

epilogue: leaving a legacy

"EVERY DAY I TRY TO LIVE MY LIFE IN SUCH A WAY THAT I ACCOMPLISH AT LEAST ONE THING THAT WILL OUTLIVE ME AND LAST FOR ETERNITY."

—VERNON BREWER

My mission statement has radically changed my life. Living its truth is almost an obsession. I evaluate everything I do with eternity in mind. This statement has forced me to ask the hard questions in life—to make sure I am spending what little time I have left on important things, things that will last for eternity.

I don't know if my perspective is because I'm getting older or because I survived cancer and realize how short and precious life can be. Maybe it's because I'm a grandfather—four times now. Regardless of the reason, I want my life to matter. I want to leave a legacy! I want to provide *help for today and hope for tomorrow* to the world's lost and hurting people.

"Go and make disciples of all nations" was the last command Jesus gave to His disciples. Jesus didn't ask us to do the impossible. He would not have commissioned us to go *to the ends of the earth* with His Gospel unless He expected us to obey.

God, You know my heart. You know my strengths and especially my weaknesses.

Thank You for allowing me to join You in helping to build Your Kingdom. Thank You for prolonging my life by healing me from cancer— to serve You. Thank You for allowing me the opportunities to see firsthand the things of this world that break Your heart . . . poverty in its extreme, disease at its worst, hunger as I've never known, and millions of people dying without You. Thank You for the privilege to be in the presence of such humble servants who are doing an incredible work for You.

You have changed my life! Don't ever let me lose sight of what's important to You! Help me to be sensitive to Your moving and to where You want me to go. Help me not to look inside, but to look upward. Give me strength; don't let me grow weary.

Thank You for giving me the wisdom to step out by faith and not listen to the hundreds of reasons why I shouldn't. Help me not to seek the recognition of man, but to cast Your vision in such a dynamic and powerful way that others can see the incredible needs of this world and be moved to do something about it. Keep me humble and on my knees as I seek You daily.

Each day may I do something for You that will outlive me and last for eternity.

Amen.

endnotes

1   Catullus, http://creativequotations.com/one/1690.htm.
2   C.S. Lewis, http://www.quotedb.com/quotes/594.
3   Dr. Paul Brand, Philip Yancey, *Fearfully and Wonderfully Made*, Grand Rapids, MI: Zondervan, 1987.
4   Matthew 9:36, NKJV.
5   Ronald Reagan, "Remarks at the Brandenburg Gate," West Berlin, Germany, 12 June, 1987.
6   R. Wayne Willis, *Today's Christian*, November/December, 1998, http://www.christianitytoday.com/tc/8r6/8r6020.html.
7   Matthew 25:40.
8   Billy Graham, http://thinkexist.com/quotation/god_has_given_us_two_hands-one_to_receive_with/296925.html.
9   Lawrence Elliott, *Reader's Digest*, September, 1991, 73-78.
10 The Jesus Film Project, http://www.jesusfilm.org/progress/statistics.html.
11 U.S. Center for World Missions, http://www.uscwm.org/.
12 Tom White, "Who are the Enemies of Christ," *The Voice of the Martyrs Special Issue*, Bartlesville, OK, 2002.
13 Matthew 16:18, KJV.
14 William Carey, http://thinkexist.com/quotes/william_carey.
15 Dietrich Bonhoeffer, http://www.worldofquotes.com/author/Dietrich-Bonhoeffer/1/index.html.
16 St. Francis of Assisi, http://thinkexist.com/quotes/st._francis_of_assisi/.
17 J. Vernon McGee, http://www.geocities.com/cobblestoneministries/2007/FamousPreacherQuotes_part3.html.
18 Alan Weber, ed. and trans., *Because It's There: A Celebration of Mountaineering from 200 B.C. to Today*, Lanham, MD: Taylor Trade Publishing, 2003.
19 Adoniram Judson, http://www.kjvuser.com/dailyquoteandverses10-01.htm.
20 Matthew 11:28.
21 John 11:26.
22 J. Hudson Taylor, http://www.sermonillustrations.com/a-z/r/risk.htm.

23   Joseph Mohr, lyrics; trans. by John F. Young (sts. 1, 2, 3) and anon.;
      Franz Gruber, music; "Stille Nacht (Silent Night)," 1816, 1818.

24   Joshua 5:9, New Century Version.

25   "Bellamy Urges Attention on Uganda's Displaced People Crisis;
      Calls on LRA to Release Children," press release, UNICEF 25 May
      2004, 14 June 2006, http://www.unicef.org/media/media_21136.html.

26   Loren Eiseley, *The Star Thrower*, Fort Washington, PA: Harvest Books, 1979.

27   Dale Hanson Bourke, *The Skeptic's Guide to the Global AIDS Crisis*,
      Waynesboro, GA: Authentic Media, 2006, 15.

28   Ibid.

29   "Fighting AIDS," The Global Fund,
      http://www.theglobalfund.org/en/about/aids.

30   Avert.org, http://www.avert.org/aidsorphans.htm.

31   Maggie Fox, "AIDS will create 40 million orphans—U.S. Report,"
      Reuters News Media, Inc., 19 Nov. 1997, http://www.aegis.com/
      news/re/1997/RE971112.html.

32   Julia Post, "'14 Million Dreams': The Compelling Stories of 5 Children
      Orphaned by AIDS in Africa," 1 Dec. 2003, Global Health Council,
      http://www.globalhealth.org/news/article/3792.

33   David Kinnamon and Fermi Project, *unChristian: What a New Generation
      Really Thinks about Christianity . . . and Why It Matters*, Grand Rapids, MI:
      Baker Books, 2007, 95.

34   Dr. Paul Brand and Philip Yancey, *Fearfully and Wonderfully Made*,
      Grand Rapids, MI: Zondervan, 1987.

35   Bono, "Transcript: Bono remarks at the National Prayer Breakfast,"
      2 February, 2006, http://www.usatoday.com/news/
      washington/2006-02-02-bono-transcript_x.htm.